Mr. Wilson

MAKES IT HOME

Michael Morse

MAKES IT HOME

How One Little Dog Brought Us Hope, Happiness, and Closure

MICHAEL MORSE

Foreword by
CHERYL MORSE

Skyhorse Publishing

Skyhorse Publishing books may be purchased in bulk at special discounts for sales promotion, corporate gifts, fund-raising, or educational purposes. Special editions can also be created to specifications. For details, contact the Special Sales Department, Skyhorse Publishing, 307 West 36th Street, 11th Floor, New York, NY 10018 or info@skyhorsepublishing.com.

Skyhorse® and Skyhorse Publishing® are registered trademarks of Skyhorse Publishing, Inc.®, a Delaware corporation.

Visit our website at www.skyhorsepublishing.com.

10 9 8 7 6 5 4 3 2 1

Library of Congress Cataloging-in-Publication Data is available on file.

Cover design by Brian Peterson
Cover photo by Robert Booth

Print ISBN: 978-1-62914-573-0
Ebook ISBN: 978-1-63220-055-6

Printed in the United States of America

CONTENTS

For Cheri Tripp
Thank you for rescuing Mr. Wilson and making our lives richer. Arkansas may be hundreds of miles away from Rhode Island, but with Mr. Wilson between us, we will always be close.

ACKNOWLEDGMENTS

To my friend and mentor, Jon Ford; the people who brought Mr. Wilson home—Jeff and Kelly O'Brien and everybody at Alpha Dog Transport; the team at Friends of Homeless Animals, RI; Ann Moan Martini, who gave me my first writing assignments; and my editor at Skyhorse Publishing, Nicole Frail. Thank you all!

FOREWORD

Several birthdays had come and gone. There was always a card from Michael, and inside a small handwritten note with soulful words expressing that indeed love was still there and always would be. And really, it was. Most times there was nothing much from me. Michael always came through with a gift; maybe from a small unusual gift store he passed on a rescue run in Providence. I usually failed when it came to that. Everyone knew it was hard for me to get around, so no one questioned it.

I've often wondered if I used my decreased mobility as an excuse to remain detached. I hope not. Internet shopping was an option that I usually ignored. I'm sad about that when I think of it now but this year I felt different, and I think Michael did too. Many things had changed during his twenty-two-year career as a Rescue Lieutenant and then Rescue Captain in a busy city fire department in Providence, Rhode Island. He often worked seventy-two-hour weeks for us. It all came to an end after years of straining his back from heavy lifting and various other things that came with such a job.

Getting to know each other again and finding a comfort level with who we were now was a challenge, but things were becoming more comfortable. I wanted his upcoming birthday to be special.

I wanted him to know that I was aware of the losses he (we) had experienced throughout the past few years. It was time to close some old wounds.

Leaving our big, yellow cape-style home, which we both loved and had spent many years turning into what we thought looked like a country cottage, was more emotional than we had anticipated. We furnished much of it with pieces and things from old consignment shops; the kind that sells so-called diamonds in the rough.

People's memories were for sale, sometimes heaped in the back of an old barn. Often we would find a part of a lamp, or a table missing a drawer, or just simply a drawer, and buy it. Michael would laugh at the mish-mash I thought was worthy of carting home. Many things we picked up had most likely been placed on the side of the road, intended for the dump, but by the end our efforts, they often would be reborn or remade into a memory that became part of our life in that home.

Leaving our neighbors Bob and Tara was difficult; the gate that connected our backyards had brought us together often rather than keeping each other out. Monday was card game night and having the gate made carting snacks that much easier. Our pool was always open to their family. Michael had few close friends, due to his schedule I guess, but Michael and Bob had grown to be best friends, always ready to help each other out. Tara and I were house-proud; we always exchanged recipes and had reached a comfort level I don't often experience with others. Card night was entertaining; not too much card-playing, but always lots to eat, some wine, and the conversations about the kids, whose activities provided us with endless stories. Our kids were high school and college age, theirs elementary, junior high and high school, so our stories gave them something to look forward to, you might say.

The move also affected our two big old dogs, who were uprooted from the only home they had ever known. We always thought they would be put to rest at that home, but because of difficulty going up and down stairs, it became apparent that a one-level house was a wise choice. We thought we could transform our next house into a place that felt like home, like we did with the yellow one. But two houses with a rental in-between were far from what we had envisioned. The dogs were put to sleep a short time after we moved into the second home. I always felt adjustment of the moves took a toll on their tired old bones. I've always felt guilty about uprooting them and us.

Being responsible for another dog wasn't something I wanted to take on again or thought I could, but life is not all about me. This time it was about taking a chance and putting a little skip in my husband's walk, and I mean that both literally and figuratively. Walking was part of a health routine advised by his physician. I knew walking itself was fairly boring, but walking alone was more so, especially when he spent twelve years walking two huge dogs who brought attention wherever they went. That is what he had lost some four years ago, his walking buddies, his pals. That's the one thing about pets—we usually outlive them.

So on a peaceful Saturday morning, I sat in front of my computer searching for the one thing I never planned on having again, "a dog." Not a big dog, not a hairy dog, and not a yappy one. I am the kind of person who decides to do something, digs in, and gets it done. I started with Pet Finder. A zip code or state is all you need, and it will show you all the available dogs in your area. Page after page, I looked and bookmarked all the dogs I thought would suit us. I was nervous the whole time that this could be a big mistake. Michael is a six-foot-three gentle giant who never yells and usually gives in to whatever the girls or I want. From what I'd read, I knew that taking the alpha position with dogs would be important, and I wondered if he was up to the task, but I had a good feeling about this. I wanted this for him, for us.

When you have lost the ability to run and open the door and let the pup out, or navigate quickly to avoid the mishaps of a pup, you really have to think about who will ultimately take charge. Later that day, when we both had down time, I called him in to show him my search results and get a feel for how he felt about my birthday gift to him. At first I'm sure he thought it was a fun idea, but that I never would really go through with it. He looked interested but hesitant. He went along, anyway. I already knew which little fellow I thought we should look into adopting, but it was his birthday, after all. We looked at the computer screen and he pointed out a couple he liked, but the dog bookmarked "number one" ultimately got his okay. We ended the day, went to sleep, and the next day I called the number attached to this scruffy, dirty white dog named Wilson.

The woman who I spoke with was from the Rhode Island Friends of Homeless Animals Association. Her name was Roie. She explained that the dog was in Arkansas and in a foster home now but arrangements would be made to have him delivered by transport on the next trip coming in from the south if all the criteria were met. She gave me the name of the woman in Arkansas who was in charge of that FOHA organization and told me to call her to find out any information I would need. I started to wonder if this was bigger than I thought, but will admit I was intrigued by the whole idea of such a group of people engaged in the rescue of animals. Animal Planet is one of my favorite TV stations and I watched many shows that focused on the circumstances of dogs in the south and the many puppy mills that exist there.

On the next phone call, I spoke with a woman named Carol Johnson who gave me the number of the foster mom who was taking care of Wilson. Another day went by before I got up the nerve to call, as this was one step further into the reality that we would have a dog again. It was late morning and I sat in front of the computer screen with the picture of Wilson on it and dialed the number.

Michael had been outside, and part of me wanted him to stay there so if the call was not what I had expected, I could forget my crazy idea. As the phone rang, Michael walked in, so I motioned for him to come in and sit. I put the phone on speaker just as I heard the voice on the other end. A woman answered with a happy, robust, Southern droll and we both looked at each other with big smiles, smiles we hadn't exchanged in a long time. We listened, somewhat giggly, as she told us all about Wilson and how she became his foster mom. We asked very few questions; it just didn't seem necessary. The feeling was all good; it felt right; it felt exciting. That day I saw a part of Michael that I hadn't seen in a long time: a pleasant contentment.

So begins the story of the dog we call Mr. Wilson.

—Cheryl Morse
September 2014

INTRODUCTION

On a brisk April morning, a parking lot full of people waited expectantly for the dogs they had adopted from various animal rescue organizations to arrive. We were together but separate—families, couples, single men and women bonded by the humanity that compelled us to adopt homeless dogs. Anticipation filled the air moments before the red tractor trailer appeared and our dogs arrived.

Then, the magic began. A collective happy-to-be-alive moment, which lasted well over an hour, enveloped us as our dogs were delivered. Afterward, we went our separate ways, each holding onto the precious memories of those moments as well as the parts of our lives that had previously been missing. For the dogs, their four-day trip from "down south" was over. For us, the journey had just begun.

Too often we bask in the negativity that surrounds us and dwell on the things that didn't happen or should have happened. But unplanned, unexpected, and unbelievable moments do happen. Periodic feelings of bliss can grab us by the throat, shake us to the core, clear our sight, and give us the clarity of mind and presence of body to stop everything, breathe deeply, turn toward the sun, feel its warmth on our skin, and bask in the moment that good fortune has given us. To feel it, acknowledge it, know that it is true, and accept the moment as a gift to be treasured is the most important thing a person can do. Letting something great pass us by without acknowledging the moment is life squandered. I will never forget the moment that Mr. Wilson arrived, for it was perfect.

Mr. Wilson Makes It Home is about love, loss, and hope. It has moments of hilarity and heartbreak, training tips for dogs and humans, compassion, giving, taking, eating, laughing, and appreciating the rare moments of grace that make our existence not simply worthwhile, but magnificent.

The gifts we received the day we brought Mr. Wilson home far exceed the simple acquisition of a pet and all the fun that goes with it. My hope for you is that you will see a glimpse of yourselves in our story, and if something is missing in your lives, may it open your heart to the idea of bringing a pet home or, if you already have one, perhaps adopting another.

PART I: THE PRESENT

Chapter 1

DESIGNER DOGS

When Cheryl decided to get us a dog, nothing could stop her. She made her mind up on a Wednesday; ten days later, on a brisk but beautiful Sunday morning, I held a twelve-pound pooch in my arms. He was a mutt, or at least what used to be considered a mutt, and he melted into my body as though he belonged there, his tired brown eyes barely open and his heart beating away. I thanked the man who handed him off to me and then turned my eyes toward my wife, who leaned on our car, capturing images of random moments with her camera. She smiled, and I smiled, and Wilson opened those eyes of his completely, and he smiled too.

We used to call them mutts, now we call dogs like him "designer dogs." I think the mutts in my life would get a kick out of that designation; they certainly acted as though they were created by design rather than by misfortune. Mutts were everywhere when

I was a kid in the seventies; spaying was not high on a family's list of priorities. Packs of dogs ran free in the neighborhoods of my town, and nobody really minded. Cardboard signs with the words FREE PUPPIES and an arrow leading to the bounty were a common sight. The signs would be nailed onto wooden phone poles by boys who prowled the neighborhood streets on bicycles equipped with monkey handlebars and banana seats—one hand holding the hammer and signs, the other keeping the bike headed in the right direction, a pocketful of roofing nails poking their skin and no helmets on their heads, but they somehow managed. If your dog had a litter, you would give the pups six weeks to grow, put up the signs, and then give them away.

The mutt that Cheryl found for us is a schnoodle; half poodle and half schnauzer, which is the best of the two breeds combined. Schnoodles are as smart as poodles, strong-willed as schnauzers, clever and active like poodles, and affectionate, like schnauzers. They are great hunting dogs, can retrieve prey, herd, protect, play the piano, and, best of all, they don't shed.

For a designer dog, Wilson got off to a rough start. His was no life of privilege. There are places where people treat dogs like revenue producers and operate businesses that some call puppy farms, or mills. As their name implies, dogs are treated like cash crops and live in filthy cages. They never run, or play, or feel what it is like to be loved, cherished, and adored by a human. They may spend their days in severe hot or cold temperatures, for it matters not to the people who farm the dogs. They are fed the bare minimum and are diseased and malnourished, but their puppies look good. The public's insatiable appetite for cute puppies keeps these places going, churning out litter after litter, until the female dogs are unable to deliver, and they are disposed of, or the males lose interest in reproducing, and they disappear.

The dog that now nestled in my arms and had already capti-vated me came from such a place. It was hard to believe—he seemed perfect, happy to be alive, and not the product of such a harsh environment. But he was, and now he wasn't. Somewhere in Arkansas lives, or lived, a poodle and a schnauzer, and their lives have one purpose and one purpose only. Their living conditions are deplorable, and they live in misery, but manage to produce stock for the nation's pet stores and Internet sites that sell their offspring for a decent profit. Volume is the way to make the most money, so they are forced to pump out as many revenue producers as nature will allow. And so do the other thousands of prisoners that exist in these places. But they make cute puppies . . .

Somebody bought this one, our new dog, in a pet store and then cast him aside when they realized that owning a dog equals a lot of work.

Most of us have learned to be more responsible pet owners, and many people see the value in having our pets spayed and neutered. People are inherently good, and kind, and when presented with the overwhelming data that supports the practice of spaying and neutering, they willingly get on board. By doing so, the supply side of the supply-and-demand equation for free puppies is a little lacking and opportunists abound.

I guess the days of the Free Puppy signs on pieces of cardboard are over. Sometimes progress isn't all that great. But my new dog certainly appeared to be, and I couldn't believe how good it felt to hold him. Cheryl had taken a leap of faith in getting him, and her gesture was not lost on me. We weren't simply getting a dog. We were affirming our bond, our commitment to each other, and our willingness to move forward into an unknown, unpredictable future. His presence in our lives had the potential to create a cohe-siveness that had been missing for far too long.

Chapter 2

MEETING

Cheryl knew me better than I knew myself, and she saw changes in me, just a few months after retiring from my job as a Rescue Captain with the Providence, Rhode Island, fire department. I wasn't aware of any changes; all I knew was that I just wasn't as tired. It had been a long twenty-two years, and the job took me away from home for far too long. I think I lost myself during that time, and Cheryl knows that I did.

There is more to life than work and dogs, and our troubles went deeper than the obvious, but getting rid of work, or rather, too much work, and bringing a dog back into our lives would give us a chance to repair what was once a great relationship but had turned sour from lack of attention. For any relationship to thrive, there needs to be two willing participants, both present and willing to do the work to maintain it. She knew that though we would never "get over" the loss of our previous dogs Zimba and Lakota, it was time to get on with our lives, and a new dog was a great place to start. Left up to me, the decision to get a new dog would have never been made; it was just something that I thought unlikely to happen, and I was afraid to open old hurts.

I should have known that when something doesn't seem likely—and owning another dog was high on the list of things unlikely to happen—chances are that something good is likely going to happen, thanks to Cheryl. It's just that way with us, and has been for the last thirty years. Thirty years? It seems like yesterday.

Thirty years ago, Cheryl was a woman with two young daughters who left an unhappy marriage after ten years, found a job waitressing at a nice restaurant, and began her new life. She had to sell her house, which had an apartment upstairs that she moved into. It must have been difficult living in the apartment you used to own, but the people who bought her home were close friends who loved Danielle and Brittany as if they were their own children. It was truly a blessing the girls were able to sleep in their own beds at night while their mother worked to support them. David and Michaela got more than a house when they moved into Cheryl's home; they gained a family.

I was a bartender at the restaurant, saw the new waitress, and was immediately smitten. It was a busy place, and she had exaggerated her experience while applying for the job, not knowing that the charm that exuded from her pores had landed her the position before the manager had even looked at her résumé. She was in over her head, but it didn't matter; the people at the restaurant wanted her to succeed.

We grew close, and I helped her garnish her drinks while the bar crowd behind me demanded theirs, but I ignored them so I could teach her to put a cherry in a Manhattan and a lime in a margarita, not the other way around. They were small things, but without them the drinks would be all wrong. She appreciated the extra attention, and I couldn't help myself. We became friends, and when the gang went out after work, we ended up together, dancing at the clubs, talking in the parking lot of the restaurant when the partying was over and the rest of the crew went their separate ways, staying up late, getting to know each other's dreams and realities.

Time progressed and we became inseparable and started our lives together. We would leave work at midnight; when the gang went to their clubs and parties, we would veer off together and often end up at our favorite spot, Conimicut Point, a small beach in our hometown, and walking in the sand under the moonlight. I taught her to skim stones across the still surface of the water, and we watched the tides ebb and flow under the pale moonlight. Sometimes we would sit in an empty lifeguard chair high above the sand, hold hands, and share soft kisses that became more passionate as the weeks of our friendship grew to months, and our lives became forever entwined.

Chapter 3

PEOPLE AND ANIMALS

The stages of life come and go without us seeing the gradual changes in ourselves that living brings. I had been miserable for some time and never even knew it. I thought I was fine, and that everybody was much like I was—a cynical, depressed fool. I don't know when it started, or when it stopped, but Cheryl did. She also saw me coming back; she liked what she saw, felt some relief, and hoped that our dark ages had passed. I started to see the world and people in it the way I used to, before my job brought me to places I never could have imagined. With each passing day, I felt my optimism returning and began letting go of the resentments and cynicism that had crept up on me.

In a blink, our lives had progressed from two kids in love to two people in their fifties, still in love, but struggling. Time has a way of wearing a person down and, as it progresses, the windows of opportunity close, one by one, until there are more years behind you than ahead. Finding the blissful serenity that true love brings can be elusive. Love is funny; we like to think the adult version is the real deal, and kids don't know anything about it, but I distinctly remember being a kid and love was most definitely the real deal. I felt harder, and hurt harder, and the joy that made the pain worth the trouble was more intense when I was young and everything was new. I missed the intensity I once felt and thought it was gone forever.

One thing that makes older love almost as good as the younger version are the memories that build as time progresses and having the ability to conjure up lost emotions elicited from those memories with a simple act of recollection. There are plenty of windows to be opened, and plenty that should stay closed, because some moments of recall can hurt. We had plenty of memories, some better than others, and plenty of pets to help us make them. Now, we had another, and some time to make the future more than time spent living in the past.

Animals are great, but we need other people to be human. As great as our pets are, or can be, they will never be able to take the place of human companionship. There is a lot to be learned from living with a dog, or a cat, but we learn everything by sharing our lives with other people. There are people, and there are animals, and we need each other, but the animals need us a little more. There's nothing better, though, than adding a dog that comes with no baggage, no expectations, and no resentment into a troubled relationship. And best of all, one who doesn't even know he needs us at all.

There was a dog out there, somewhere, just waiting for us to find him and bring him home. Cheryl found ours by searching the way just about everybody finds just about everything: she did a Google search. Things happen fast on the information super-highway, and it didn't take long to turn the pixels on our computer screen into reality. A homeless dog was adopted by two dog-less people, and two dog-less people were adopted by the homeless dog. Our little guy was thousands of miles away when Cheryl first saw his little face. And then thousands of miles were eclipsed, just like that!

Of course, there is more to the story. Doing anything worthwhile is difficult, and getting our new dog from there to here did not magically just happen. Procedures were in place; volunteers standing by; phone calls, emails, veterinary appointments, drop-offs and pick-ups, and deposits were made; there were inspections, paperwork, background checks; and on and on. People are behind this remarkable network—good, loving, dedicated people, worthy of every human being's respect.

Great things do not just happen. People make them happen, and it's hard work with no monetary reward. Money can't buy a person love and happiness, but the evidence of love and happiness being available for free happened right before our eyes.

Chapter 4

STARFISH

Cheryl's internet search for dogs for adoption in Rhode Island led her to a place called Petfinder, and true to the name of the site, we found our pet. Knowing nothing about the complicated, fragile, and remarkable pipeline that existed for these homeless animals, she thought the pictures flashing across her screen were of dogs close by, perhaps as near as the local animal shelter. Rhode Island is a small state, the smallest of the fifty, but has no shortage of shelters. Each of the state's thirty-nine cities or towns has their own government, their own police department, fire department, and school. Most have their own animal shelters as well, and a number of private places join the municipal facilities for a total of sixty-three shelters in a state you can drive through in less than an hour. There are a lot of homeless animals under our noses, and we wanted to give one another chance.

Roie Griego started Friends of Homeless Animals of RI (FOHARI) as a rescue organization that found homes for unwanted Boston terriers. But that is far from how Roie began rescuing animals. Her work has taken her to places that most of us can barely imagine. The suffering that exists in the animal kingdom is staggering and unnecessary.

For some, animal rescue is a passion, and they devote their lives to making the world we live in a better place because of the work they do. Some may ask, "Why bother rescuing unwanted pets and animals when there is so much need in the human population?" I have asked the same questions, never giving enough thought to the answer.

After talking with Roie, the answer became clear. We rescue animals because, by doing so, we help both people and the animals who inhabit this earth at the same time we do. It humbles me to think that in one hundred years, nearly every person or animal alive right now will be gone. The animals cannot take care of themselves, and people are directly affected by the health and well-being of the animals. Spending time in Mexico, working to improve the lives of abandoned and feral animals there, Roie learned that even the smallest contribution to lessening the enormity of the homeless pet problem is a worthy undertaking. Her work with stray street dogs was the catalyst for Veterinarians Without Borders, whose mission statement is: "Veterinarians Without Borders advances human health and livelihoods in underserved areas by sustainably improving veterinary care and animal husbandry, working toward preventing, controlling and eliminating priority diseases. Our Vision: Enhance human and animal health and create a secure, diverse, and healthy food supply for all the world's people."

I asked Roie how she remains dedicated after seeing so much misery. She has been an activist for more than thirty years, has worked with the Audubon Society showing children the value of wildlife at the Blue Hills Trailside Museum in Massachusetts, and was involved with Jacques Cousteau's "Involvement Days." She lived in Texas and became the chair of a local Boston terrier group's rescue division, which in all likelihood led her to her work as the president of FOHARI.

"The story of the starfish describes it best," she said, and I waited for her to continue, knowing from the brief time that we shared talking on the phone that this was a special person, and the story that would follow worthy of hearing. "A man walked along the beach, and millions of starfish had washed ashore. He bent over, and over, tossing them back into the ocean so that they might live a little longer. A different man walked toward him, stopped when he saw what was going on, and asked the man throwing the fish back into the ocean why he bothered when so many would be left to die in the sand or be washed back ashore. What difference did it make? The man who had been throwing the starfish back in the ocean stopped what he was doing, looked at the living creature in his hand, and said, 'Because to this starfish, it makes all the difference.' And he threw the starfish into the ocean, and bent over and picked up another."

All the pets FOHA helps are kept in foster homes until somebody notices them, usually through the Internet, but sometimes at adoption events. Local pet stores and many pet supply chains have gotten on board, foregoing the practice of selling puppies in lieu of holding adoption events. Different animal rescue groups come together and hold an adoption festival, the foster pets are all brought to a central location, and people looking to adopt can look around and find their perfect pet.

I never knew any of this. It was inconceivable to me that thousands of people cared for dogs in their homes so that somebody else could adopt them. I had spent the last twenty-plus years working as an EMT in Providence. My world revolved around sick people, injured people, dead and dying people, and people who had given up hope. There was an occasional happy ending to a 911 call, but the negative outcomes far exceeded the positive. It is a difficult environment in which to stay optimistic, and I fell into the deep end of the pool of disillusionment head first.

Simply knowing that people with whom I share this Earth find the time, empathy, and hope within themselves to chip away at the immense problem of unwanted pets opened my eyes to the possibility that perhaps there is a better way, and closing the doors of my mind on the problem was not necessarily a very good coping mechanism. My job made me good at taking care of sick and injured people. It was time for my life to veer toward taking care of myself, my family, and maybe even some homeless pets.

Chapter 5

CATS

Wilson would not be our first pet, nor would he be our first adopted pet. A house without a pet—or at least fond memories of one—is not a home, I always say. I love the way the little critters give a house personality. In many ways, our homes are more homes to the pets that live there than they are to us. We are part-time members in our houses, most days spending only half of our waking hours there, some days even less than that. Our pets never leave. They never complain about not getting away. Most don't go on vacations or trips to the mall. For the most part, they stay put and are happy at home. Some might go on a poorly conceived dash through the neighborhood every now and then, imagining themselves as wild as their ancestors and impulsively darting out of an open door or digging under a fence, grasping their need to run free, but they always come to their senses and find their way home. Sometimes it only takes a minute;

sometimes it takes longer than they had planned. Some never make it home at all and become homeless pets. But, in general, they stay home, and they like it just fine.

We were just about ready to move forward with our plan of adopting a dog, but were not 100 percent comfortable with our decision. We were at maybe 95 percent. There were just too many things that could go wrong. Adopting or buying a pet is a commitment and, for better or worse, the rule. Once we made the commitment, there would be no turning back because it wasn't working. If we lived our lives turning back when the going got tough, we would have been living separate lives by now. Relationships are work, plain and simple, and owning a pet is a relationship, make no mistake.

Sometimes, what seems to be a great idea turns out to be not so great. Take Victoria. She is a wonderful animal, very easy on the eyes, gentle when she wants to be and an absolute bitch when she doesn't—which is most of the time. We adopted her from a cat rescue organization eight years ago.

"She sure is pretty," I said to Cheryl after the lady who had dropped her off abruptly left.

"When you can see her," she replied, watching her tail disappear around a corner.

"She is fast, that's for sure. Never seen a cat move so quick."

"What's she running from?"

"I have no idea."

We still have no idea. She spooks easily, has a tendency to hide under a chair all day, and likes nothing more than to escape into our unfinished basement and eat bugs. On occasion, she will jump onto my lap, turn and lie on her back, and purr like a Harley Davidson.

"She might be feral," Cheryl said one day when Victoria leapt four feet into the air from a lying position and flew out of the room.

"I think her mother and father are brother and sister."

"She might have eaten lead paint when she was a kitten."

"Or fell on her head."

More likely she was abused at some point in her life. It doesn't take much to turn a loving, trusting kitten into a half-squirrel, half-cat. Victoria came to us at a year old, and we had hoped that she would fill the void that the passing of the Greatest Cat in the World, Sabrina, had left when kidney disease took her from us at eight years old.

Sabrina was another castaway, coming by way of the friendship railroad. A friend of our oldest daughter, Danielle, thought he would win her affection by bringing her a kitten.

She sure loved that kitten. We're not quite sure what happened to her friend.

We think she was a full-blooded Maine Coon cat and was barely six weeks old when we got her. She lived with us from that point on, loving all of us, but seldom leaving Cheryl's side. She never complained and was playful, smart, kind, and had a little pink nose and what looked like white eyeliner highlighting her beautiful, soulful eyes.

She fit in nicely with our other cats at the time—Tasha, who was without question the queen, Magick, and Allie. Magick was funny, plain and simple. Her head was too small for her body, and she was jet-black with tiny little feet that carried her like a rocket out an open door and into the great world beyond, where she would stop five feet after escaping and eat grass until somebody went out and brought her back. She loved Brittany, our younger daughter, and was devoted to her exclusively. She liked the rest of us okay, and was nice for the most part, but she lived for Brittany's company.

Allie loved Christmas. She waited all year for the tree to make its annual pilgrimage from the basement and would lie under it as soon as it was up, decorated or not. Typically, our house was void of presents under the tree until a few days before Christmas, but Allie didn't mind, and looked like the best present in the world when she slept under the tree and basked in the soft glow from those little lights. Every now and then she would climb the tree, but we didn't mind, and it only took a little while to stand it up and put things right when she was done.

They all died too young, Magick from congestive heart failure and Allie from a blood infection. Little Sabrina had kidney failure, and we gave her syringes full of lactated ringers for a year before she left us. They were an important part of our family, and we remember them often, though not as often as we did shortly after they passed. Seldom does a month go by when somebody doesn't mention one of them, or all.

Tasha, our original and by far the most ferocious of all of our companions, is remembered fondly as well. She was a gray cat that caught snakes and left them on our doorstep. But she was nice, too, and would snuggle on top of our water heater and wait for somebody to pet her. She only made it to fourteen, and I wish she lived for twenty.

But Victoria? She's nine years old and will live to be thirty, I'm sure. She's making progress, and as we are fond of mentioning when she rips open our flesh and makes a petrified dart from our lap or arms, "she's come a long way."

If we adopted a dog, and it certainly appeared as though we were about to, we would be responsible for him for the remainder of his days, no matter how long that would be. He might be mean, or skittish, or untrainable, or bark all day and all night, or bite, or puke without warning, or . . . we just didn't know.

But we were about to find out.

Chapter 6

CHERI

Wilson looked like a great dog, but can a picture take the place of a thousand words? I've seen many photographs of charming boys and girls who look angelic in their First Communion clothes, or Easter best, but in real life are absolute monsters. Our family photo albums are full of such pictures, and our family full of such monsters. When I break out the volumes full of memories and take a walk back in time, I am amazed at how wonderful my brother and sisters and I look in the old Polaroids, and how angelic Brittany and Danielle appear in the more recent but already antiquated Kodak film.

Cheri, the person fostering Wilson until he found a forever home, lived in Arkansas and knew him best. We had gotten Cheri's phone number from the people at FOHARI and decided to give her a call, just to see if she would tell us a little something about him. The instant we made this connection, all of our doubts and fears about our new dog went away. Speaking with Cheri was like talking with an old, dear friend. She loved our New England accents, and we loved her Southern drawl, and none of us even knew we spoke any different from everybody else!

She told us all about Wilson, how he was a love bug, and when needed most would "love you up!" She described an intelligent, fun-loving, and kind animal, one who acted nearly human, for a dog, and she let us know that if something happened and we couldn't take care of Wilson, she would drive to Rhode Island and take him back to Arkansas.

Cheryl and I sat on our bed, with Cheri on speakerphone, and a warm glow filled the room, emanating from the tinny sound from the telephone speaker, which Cheri managed to make magical. Her musical way of speaking, and the kindness that was expressed by her words, left us no doubt whether we were doing the right thing by adopting Wilson. She loved that dog, and hearing her describe their relationship nearly broke our hearts. Here was a good woman who had found a good friend, but due to her circumstances, she had decided to do her best and find that friend a good home. It must have been heartbreaking for her to let him go.

Listening to Cheri describe her life in Arkansas was the most relaxing, honest moment we had had in a long, long time. She easily conveyed a sense of calm—a more measured pace to life— and an appreciation of family, the Earth and a little dog that needed a break. We heard about Alene, Cheri's mom, who lived five acres away, and would watch Wilson while Cheri went to work cleaning the homes of the wealthy and then pull another shift at a car dealership five nights a week. Cleaning homes and car dealerships is hard work; Cheryl and I knew this, as we ran a home and office cleaning service for nearly twenty years and at one time had thirty accounts. It is exhausting and tedious, and to find the kindness in her heart to take in a stray after all the work she did on a daily basis was truly remarkable. She spoke kindly of her brother, who was enjoying success at Levi Strauss, and how she harbored no resentments and was happy for him. I couldn't help but wonder if the Levi's executive would find room in his heart and most likely sizable home like his sister did; Cheri's home is small, but her heart is bigger than her neighboring state of Texas. I think that he would. Something runs in family blood. Every now and then, somebody goes astray, but family is family, and it is difficult to stray too far from the values imbedded in us by our genetic makeup and upbringing.

We reluctantly ended our call with Cheri and sat back feeling better than we had in a very long time. Wilson had not yet begun his journey north, but his influence was already working wonders in two people he had never met.

I asked Cheri if she could pass on a little more information about Wilson.

She did:

My first encounter with Wilson was in November 2012. He and his sister had escaped from their owners and had been on the run for several days. I looked everywhere for their owners but to no avail. I finally gave them a bath and fed them and went to work, leaving them with my mother, who already had two Cairn terriers and my Yorkie to care for, so she now had five dogs in the house with her.

After work I took Trouble a.k.a. Wilson and his sister to my 10x15 ft. house and we all nestled in for the night. The next day, after speaking with some neighbors, I finally found their home and took them back to their owners. That's when I found out from their owner that Wilson was his name and he belonged to her son, who wasn't around much. She told me that Wilson was always running off.

So from that point on, I always kept my eyes open for Wilson. There are dogs everywhere in the county. No one keeps their dogs in a gate or fence, so you have to be very careful when going to town. In December, Wilson escaped again and I took him back again. There were several escapes and returns through February.

In March, around the 24th, we were coming home from Cracker Barrel and, as we turned down our street, the Holy Spirit literally tapped me on the shoulder and told me to go check on Wilson. So I backed up and headed for their house. When I got there, the owner told me Wilson was in the barn and that she couldn't keep him from escaping so she put him out there. He was wet and cold, no food or blankets, and his whiskers were frozen, so I picked him up, looked at my mom, and put him in her lap.

I took him home and fed and loved him because he was scared, shaking, and lost inside from her mean actions. The weather was 34 degrees and raining. He settled in nicely, but he kept digging his way out of our fence. I placed rocks, bricks, and anything I could find in holes he had dug trying to get out . . . and he would still get out. Sometimes while we were on the back porch, working puzzles or reading the paper, we would look up and Wilson would be on the other side of the fence wanting back in.

Out he'd go and back in he'd want. So after two weeks of this nonsense, I finally let him and Tippy, our Yorkie, run the property. Within a few days, he quit digging and got comfortable. I finally went to Waymack Animal Clinic and put up his picture for adoption, and the next day a woman named Carol called wanting to know if she could find him a good home. I said yes.

Never in my life have I known love from a dog as I experienced with Wilson. He would jump up in the chair and lay his head on my shoulder or lick me with such warm kisses. Just plop down in my lap and go to sleep. Always very comfortable and at home wherever he was. He's easily the most affectionate dog I've ever known. I truly fell in love with Wilson and didn't want to let him go. Carol called me a couple weeks later and told me to take him back to Waymack Animal

Clinic, have him fixed and his hair shaved, and get all of his shots. So he was gone for a few days but was soon back with us and happy as a lark.

Soon thereafter, Cheryl called me about Wilson and the rest is history! He now resides in Providence, Rhode Island, has a great family who adores him, is smitten by Mike especially, and gets to go to the beach. He wears a bandanna and seems happier than any dog I know. Even my dog.

Love,
Cheri Tripp

Thank you Cheri, for letting Wilson be Wilson.

Chapter 7

A BIGGER BOAT

We spent the days between Wilson's departure from Arkansas and his arrival in Rhode Island preparing for him. Our experience with Zimba and Lakota and life with the cats had taught us all there was to know about living with dogs and cats, and we knew we were about to learn everything we thought we knew all over again. We went forward with our plan to raise and train the perfect dog. We bought a book, *How to Train a Dog Perfectly*, or something like that, and began reading in earnest. Dogs are great companions, and good friends. But they need a leader, or leaders, and that was going to be us. For this to work, we needed to be on the same page and approach training with the same mindset. Neither of us wanted a clingy dog, or a yapper, or a biting, uncontrollable nuisance, so we learned all we could prior to getting Wilson. We learned a lot over the years and loved watching TV shows that centered around dogs and the way people try to fold dogs into their way of thinking. Both of us knew that it is more often the human that needs training, not the dog.

By all accounts, well, by Cheri's accounts, Wilson was a perfect gentleman—fun loving, intelligent, and highly trainable. The rest would be up to us. For this to work, and work well, we needed to be fully prepared.

The first thing on the list was a crate. Crate training is supposedly the very best way to make sure your dog respects his home and does his business outside of it. Encapsulating that home into the size of a crate, one small enough that there is no room for waste, is a great first lesson.

"What do you think of this one?" Cheryl asked as we trudged through Wal-Mart one night, a few days prior to Wilson's arrival.

"Too big," I said, looking at the metal cage. With some modifications, it might be cozy, and I knew that Cheryl would comfy it up, but it just looked too much like a jail cell. Smaller jail cells are not as offensive to me—even less so if there is absolutely no way that I could ever fit into it. This one I just might be able squeeze into, so it was off the list. The last thing I wanted was a jail cell in my living room.

There were no appropriate crates at the store, so we filled our shopping cart with doggie dishes, leashes, runners, cookies, a squeaky chicken, and shampoo instead. There were other stores, and not being the kind of people to leave any store unturned, we began our quest, ready to cover the tri-county area in search of the perfect crate. And a better dog bowl, because we just knew one existed. And some healthy doggie treats. Organic and gluten free if possible, and if not, we would make our own.

Yup, this dog ownership thing was going to be a breeze.

We finished our journey before really getting started. Considering we started at seven at night, a proper quest was never really a possibility, but we like to kid ourselves and believe that we can do anything.

"Look at this," said Cheryl from the rear aisle of our local Job Lot store. They must have found a truckload of dog crates somewhere, because a perfectly sized and easy-to-assemble crate was right there waiting for us. It was nylon, and blue, and looked like an oversized gym bag, but it was also perfect for Wilson, especially after we purchased the little woolly bed that fit right inside.

Happy with our progress, we came home and unloaded the bounty. I couldn't wait to set up Wilson's new home inside a home, and immediately did so. I left it where I thought our new dog would like it best, right in the thick of things, in the middle of the living room.

Lunabelle, our Maine Coon cat liked it, too. She stepped right in, plopped down on the bed, and was sound asleep in seconds. She didn't leave all night.

"What are we going to do about that?" Cheryl asked when she saw the big fur ball that had invaded Wilson's new home within a home.

"I don't think there's a heck of a lot we can do," I said, knowing how difficult it is to extricate Luna from anywhere she does not wish to be extricated from. She is a real Maine Coon cat, one that we bought from a breeder eight years ago. She truly is remarkable, big, pleasant, and gorgeous—and as stubborn as a mule.

Quint from the movie *Jaws* came to mind, in particular the scene where Bruce, the great white shark that had terrorized Nantucket, nearly ate their boat. Quint assessed the damage, and leered at his companions, and then he said with a mischievous grin and Cape Cod accent, "We're gonna need a bigger boat."

Chapter 8

TIMBERCATZ

I looked at Luna, who was now firmly entrenched in her new lair and completely ignoring me, scratched my chin with my thumb and forefinger, broke out my best Cape Cod voice, and said, "We're gonna need a bigger crate." Lunabelle rolled onto her side, yawned, and went back to sleep, comfortable in her newfound home. Cheryl rolled her eyes. Quint smiled and walked away.

We bought Lunabelle from a reputable breeder who is absolutely in love with Maine Coon cats. Timbercatz is a cattery located in Massachusetts, about an hour drive away for us. We visited the place and made friends with Nellie and David, the owners. We had always adopted or just ended up with the pets that shared our lives and were a little concerned about buying a cat. Adopting is great, but we wanted a purebred. And we got one.

People have criticized our choice, claiming that we are selfish or are contributing to the problem of unwanted pets—they say that our buying a cat essentially sentenced another one to death.

Maybe they are right.

What is definitely right is the fact that we take care of our animals, and spay or neuter them, and take them to the vet, and give them all the love and protection they need and more. Lots of people don't. Lots of people let their dogs and cats have litters and try to sell the offspring or give them away when nobody buys them. They may let them escape, and then they end up in a shelter. By giving up on responsible pet owners and only taking care of the animals that have been abandoned or neglected, we are in essence giving up on ourselves. We are letting those who choose to act recklessly and in total disregard for the sanctity of pedigree, or proper breeding, dictate how we live our lives and who we will live them with.

I like living in a world where people can enter their pets in dog and cat shows, and the animals get to prance and preen and show off a little. It keeps the pets happy, and I have yet to hear of anything but well cared for and pampered pets at these shows. I like seeing an animal in all of its glory and the differences in breed celebrated. I do not want to live in a generic, blah world where everything looks the same and nothing is allowed to be different.

Lunabelle is every bit as precious and deserving of all we have to offer as responsible pet owners as Wilson, or Victoria, or any other pet that survived the school of hard knocks. Coming from a breeder doesn't make her better than an adopted pet, and it most definitely does not make her less deserving of a good life. Nellie and David are Maine Coon cat enthusiasts. The lineage of each of their cats can be traced for generations. Their cats are champions, and they proudly display the ribbons and trophies in their home.

All the cats that we saw there were well taken care of and were not allowed to leave their mother until twelve weeks of age. These are good people, and animal lovers, and protectors of those animals. They have a different philosophy concerning pet ownership and acquisition than the pet rescue people, but when you consider their love for animals is real, you see that they are not that much different at all.

Pets for adoption are not always available with exact specifications that meet the owners' needs. If you are looking for a particular breed of dog or cat and you are not able to visit the site and meet the parents of the pet you want, chances are good that you'll turn to an odd site on the Internet or a pet store to get what you want. And in that case, you may be supporting the people who operate inhumane puppy mills. Instead of essentially ordering a pet online, you should look to local breeders. They can back up their claims of ethical treatment of the pets that they sell, and they are committed to their work and the welfare of the breed.

Our experience with Luna and her family was fantastic, and I consider David and Nellie friends. We have had breakfast in their home, and met their daughter, Alyssa, who loves having a houseful of kittens, but is sad when they go. Knowing the people who buy "her" kitties makes it easier for her and staying in touch, giving progress reports, and telling stories and sharing pictures keeps things close to her heart. Breeding animals properly is a labor of love, I have learned, and not at all about profit.

Still, pet rescues are, in my opinion, the best place to find a great pet. We have always begun our searches for our pets there, and more often than not find what we were looking for. Now, with the help of the Internet, just about any breed of companion can be found, either at a shelter or in a foster home. Those resources weren't available when we got Luna, or if they were, they were rudimentary at best.

I often wonder what will happen if everybody stops buying dogs and cats from breeders. Would the breeders keep on breeding? Probably not; the supply and demand principles that dictate the market would flood the world with purebred animals and not enough people who want them. How long will it take to end the cycle? To have as many people available as pets who need them? Years? Decades?

I just don't know. I don't even know if such a thing is possible. I like to think that it is. But I would hate to see purebred dogs and cats disappear while we were busy solving the problem.

Chapter 9

LEAVING

Every Wednesday, Jeff, Kevin, and Sir (Jeff's German shepherd) begin the trek that ultimately unites homeless pets with adoptive and foster families. Their journey starts at three in the morning in Leicester, Massachusetts, where Jeff and Kelly make their home. And a busy home it is! They have six kids— age 3, 6, 7, 10, 13, and 19 years old—and a couple handfuls of dogs; both pets of their own and foster dogs. They even have cats! Sir begins pacing on Tuesday nights; his inner clock still working full time despite his age, telling him that the road is beckoning.

Every week they make the trip; there is an unending supply of dogs that need homes. They head west, drive for hours, and arrive in Mount Gilead, Ohio, between 4:30 and 5:00 in the afternoon. There they pick up dogs from various animal rescue organizations and move on, sometimes making more Ohio stops, sometimes heading straight to Indianapolis, Indiana, where they pick up more dogs at the Ramada Limited parking lot, a pre-arranged meeting place, where they rest for the night. Of course, the growing population of dogs who need attention makes that rest fitful at best.

On Thursday, it's off to Missouri, traveling through some of the most remote mountain highways in America, where moonshiners once made their fortunes. Nowadays, the distinct smell of crystal meth production enters the truck's cabin unexpectedly, as the crew journeys inland, and rugged and dangerous entrepreneurs continue the tradition of supplying the nation with illegal intoxicants. I don't think the crystal meth crowd will ever weave themselves seamlessly into the rich, colorful folklore that emanates from those parts like the moonshiners did, but life is strange, and you just never know what the future will bring.

Into the heart of Missouri with a truck full of crates—some full, but most empty—go Jeff and Kevin, stopping at the Cracker Barrel in St. Charles between 8:00 and 9:00, then on to Fenton, and another Cracker Barrel. From there, it's over to Poplar Bluff at the TAG Fuel Center at 67 South. By 3:30, it's another stop, this time at the Walnut Ridge Bowling Alley in Arkansas, and finally finishing for the day at another Cracker Barrel, this one in North Little Rock, Arkansas, where our own Wilson makes his grand appearance and joined the crew of refugees as they continue their journey.

Friday morning comes quick, and there are dogs that need transport, and the journey continues. At 7:15, the transport stops in a fireworks store parking lot in Memphis, Tennessee, and picks up a few more passengers. By nine, they are in Jackson, at Exit 79 off of Route 40, near a BP gas station. Another Cracker Barrel at ten and then more pets, this latest gang from the Dickson, Tennessee, area, gets on board.

The Grand Ole Opry is next, but there is no time for sightseeing as Jeff and Kevin pick up another crew in Nashville and are back on the road by noon, trucking down I-40 toward exit 288,

Highway 111 in Cookville. They then continue onward to Knoxville, where they arrive around three. The first part of the journey ends at McDonald's in Bullgap, Tennessee, and if all things went without a hitch, the guys would be finished by five or so.

If all things went without a hitch . . . what a wonderful world this would be.

In this world, the crew would wake before sunrise, say goodbye to their sleeping families, mount their truck, and arrive in Ohio, where they would pick up kind, gentle, well-adjusted pets at all of the pre-arranged stops. Nobody would be late, nobody would have diarrhea, the truck would run perfectly, traffic would magically make way for the important missionaries whose purpose allows them safe, untroubled passage to the promised land: McDonald's in Bullgap, Tennessee!

Well, life with Alpha Dog Transport is always an adventure. Dogs are unpredictable, people more so, traffic is a living, breathing entity that moves and slows and stops and speeds up at will, weather seldom cooperates, and mechanical difficulties abound, even in the most well-maintained vehicles. But Jeff and Kevin handle the ups and downs of the road with good humor and patience, knowing that the magical second part of the trip will make all the headaches associated with travel well worth the trouble. They have a truck full of dogs who won the lottery and are about to get second, third, or fourth chances at life. Many of those who fill the truck would have been gone in any other circumstance; they'd be ashes at the bottom of an incinerator at one of the thousands of kill shelters, or worse—living at the heel of an abusive or neglectful owner, one who treats a pet as a possession, a thing without a soul, feelings, or rights.

Animals do have rights, perhaps not the same rights as a person does (at least from a legal viewpoint), but they do have the right to live free of fear from attack by those who have agreed to provide them shelter. They should live this way. A surprising number of people consider dogs and cats as commodities, though—things to be bought and sold, given and taken at will, fed when convenient, cast out on a whim, abandoned, hurt, and left to fend for themselves or die.

The dogs that travel with Alpha Dog Transport are in the first-class section of the pet highway. Their quarters are air-conditioned and ventilated and heated when it's cold. They are fed food specific to each of their individual needs and documented by the persons who cared for them prior to the journey. Medication schedules are strictly adhered to, they are let out of their crates and allowed to stretch, and they can relieve themselves every four hours. They are touched: they get the area behind their ears scratched if they crave that kind of thing. They receive kind words and reassuring caresses if they are troubled. A sense of well-being transcends from the people who cared enough to get them on the road to new homes, through the transport, and into the hearts and souls of their new owners.

Driving a truck is easy. Well, compared to transporting a trailer full of living, breathing, thinking, and feeling cargo, it's easy. Getting a truckload full of individuals from Point A to Point B could be easy, too—if the persons doing the transporting treated their cargo like cargo rather than the way Jeff and Kevin treat theirs: like old friends who need a lift.

Chapter 10

COMING HOME

With a truckload of dogs; a load of food, fresh water, medicine; and a full tank of diesel Jeff, Kevin, and the gang begin their journey home. For Jeff and Kevin, this is a weekly journey; for the dogs, it's a once-in-a-lifetime trip. Crates filled with living creatures are secured to the trailer walls. The sleeping, restless, playful, and terrified passengers get ready for the trip north. All along the trail Alpha Dog Transport travels, groups of people gather, waiting for their packages. And what incredible packages they are!

Wilson had no idea what the future would bring, only that one minute, he was wandering around Arkansas and the next, he was chained up in a freezing barn. Then a nice lady fed him, cared for him, and he made a friend named Tippy. Now, he was in a crate and on a truck.

I had heard of people getting dogs at highway rest stops and thought the practice to be mysterious, covert, and maybe a little dangerous—definitely something I wanted to be part of. The thought of a clandestine meeting in broad daylight and exchanging living creatures with truck drivers that appeared and then disappeared into the mist sounded like something right out of a spy thriller.

The reality was even better—not as mysterious, but every bit as exciting. The idea that these prearranged drop-offs happen all the time is fascinating; it's one of those little mysteries in life that make living so interesting. Finding out that the meetings are not at all mysterious was not a letdown; it was an affirmation of the human condition—that condition being one of kindness, giving, and the ability to receive what is given. If we were not able to fully appreciate the gifts that sometimes find their way into our lives, those gifts would not mean as much and would be taken for granted and forgotten as soon as they happened.

Jeff says that doing what he does is like being Santa Claus year-round. For a Marine and retired cop, being Santa is a dream come true. Good things come to good people. You get out of life what you put into it, and what you put into it will get you what you deserve. Delivering dogs to people who want them and will do their very best to take care of them—or finding people who will—may seem an unlikely occupation for a soldier and police officer. Given the choice, though, I think most cops and soldiers would relish the opportunity to lay down their weapons when the fighting is done (or when the person is done fighting) and put it all behind them and move forward with their lives. And if that life involves a truckload full of dogs and a houseful of kids, cats, dogs, and a beautiful wife, well, all the better. Maybe even a firefighter/EMT might be inspired to leave it all behind and start a fresh new life.

There are some in the pet adoption world who disagree with the practice of adopting pets from one area and shipping them to another. "There are plenty of unwanted pets right in our own backyard," they say. And they are correct. Shelters everywhere are full of animals nobody wants. The world is full of animals nobody wants. It is miraculous that people are willing to do the work necessary to find these animals new, comfortable homes. Those people shake off the criticism of their peers and continue doing what they know is right. And in doing so, they save a lot of lives.

Cheryl wanted one of those animals that no one wanted, and she did what it took to get him. We needed a little dog that didn't shed and there were none close to us. But there was one in Arkansas, and he was on his way home.

Every four hours Jeff, Kevin, and Sir stop their vehicle and give the dogs a break. That's a lot of breaks, considering there are dozens of dogs to walk, feed, and clean up after. Shipping tomatoes or rocks would be a lot easier, but doing things easy doesn't always come with the reward that hard work does. Anything worthwhile is difficult.

Most of the time, the crew heads south and picks up adoptees, the arrangements being made through various adoption agencies and pet rescue organizations. Occasionally a dog from the north will be delivered to the southern region. Wilson is a southern boy, and his story is a little different—he never did time on death row. Cheri saved him from that fate, and now it's Jeff, Kevin, and Sir's turn. Wilson would spend the time during transport snuggled in his crate, missing Cheri but making the best of things.

The first stop on the way home is in Haggerston, Maryland, in the Toys "R" Us parking lot. The truck arrives between midnight and 1:00 am, and the fun begins. Dogs are united, people are happy, and Alpha Dog Transport moves on, the good feelings building as the trip progresses through the dark, lonely highways. At two in the morning, they roll into Harrisburg, Pennsylvania, at exit 69 off of Route 81 North. There is a Turkey Hill gas station there, and the people who run it are kind enough to set aside some time and space for the cause. Sleepy-eyed people wake at the sight of the big red truck and little trailer and are fully conscious when their new friends make their way into their hearts.

At four-thirty, when the first traces of dawn tinge the eastern sky, the truck makes another stop, this time in Parsippany, New Jersey, in the Sheraton parking lot. More introductions, more happy dogs, and more tears of joy and laughter fill the predawn air. Sir leaves the cabin when all the dogs are united with their caretakers, sniffs around, does his business, and lumbers back to Jeff and Kevin. He sleeps through sunrise as the weary travelers keep on trucking. At 7:30, with the sun shining and a new day beginning for most, the truck stops at the Stop & Shop in Waterville, Connecticut, where another emotional scene takes place. Jeff and Kevin never get enough of making people and dogs happy, and though the four days of travel and work begin to take its toll on the muscles and joints, the endorphin release—one associated with simply bearing witness to the miracle of human kindness and the instinctual response of that kindness from the dogs—provides a feeling of well-being that gallons of coffee and bags full of the crystal meth left with the cooks in the mountains behind them could never touch.

But those good feelings and well-being are not going to bring the rest of the dogs home, so it's on to Moosup/Plainfield, Connecticut, at exit 89 off of Route 395. This was Wilson's stop.

Most weeks, Jeff and Kevin arrive on Saturday morning at nine-thirty, and a dozen or so people are waiting. This specific Saturday,

Cheryl and I were among the group. Usually the stops are right on time, or close enough where time is easily made up between stops, but on Wilson's trip, some mechanical troubles delayed things by a day. So it was on a Sunday when Wilson made it home.

From there, the drivers packed up and drove off to Brattleboro, Vermont, to a parking lot behind the Burger King. People there are every bit as excited about their experience as were the folks at midnight, and so are the dogs and the dog deliverers. There is no room for tired, cranky people on this roller coaster. The same goes for the final stop in Kittery, Maine, where there is a rest stop off of I-95 North. There, the last of the dogs are delivered, and the crew finally heads home. And they do it again next week, and the week after, and the week after that.

Chapter 11

ANYTHING WORTHWHILE

While we were preparing our home for the newest member of the family, Wilson was on the road, heading north. He spent four days in the back of a truck with dozens of other dogs, each headed toward an uncertain future.

"He's going to be scared," I said to Cheryl.

"Probably take a week or two for him to settle in," she replied.

The rest area was filled with people like us—twenty or so couples, some families in groups of three or more, and a few single people were scattered around the lot on a sunny, brisk Sunday afternoon in April. Exit 89 off Route 395 was the rendezvous point, and we all waited, eagerly anticipating the new additions to our families. It was just a parking lot, but the people who filled it made it much more.

"Do you think we did the right thing?" Cheryl asked.

"I'm sure of it," I said.

Sure of it I was not. I had sworn that the only way I would ever get another dog was if somebody invented one that outlived me. Zimba and Lakota were part of our lives for a dozen years and will be forever enshrined in our family legacy. So much happened during their tenure as family guardians—our daughters Danielle and Brittany grew up, went to college, and moved away; Cheryl and I grew apart, grew together again, then began to unravel again; and we moved four times and still aren't settled. "The Dogs," as we affectionately referred to them, were with us all the way, silent observers during the unsettled period of time they shared with us. Dogs don't live forever, and part of the deal of owning a dog is having to say goodbye. It's never easy, and it takes a long time to recover when you lose one, and even longer when you lose two.

I had never expected to be holding a dog again. And I had told myself I was okay with that. We still hadn't gotten over Zimba and Lakota, and we never would. I was worn out after spending the last two decades putting out fires and patching people up while spending too much time away from home. My career as a fire-fighter/EMT had taken its toll on me and Cheryl, both emotionally and physically. Cheryl's battle with multiple sclerosis presented its own difficulties, and owning another dog hadn't seemed likely. We just didn't have much left to give, and it wouldn't be fair to the dog.

If nothing else, the last few years taught us that obtaining anything worthwhile is difficult most of the time. Things that come easily go just as easily, and I've noticed that I tend to get back exactly what I put in, effort wise. It was time, and Cheryl was the catalyst. I needed a nudge, and she was never shy when it came to giving such nudges when they were needed. I realized we were ready to do the work we knew needed to be done, put the past away, and again enjoy the companionship that only a dog can deliver. It was time to move on, while remembering to cherish the memories of dogs past.

Loving an animal can be every bit as intense as loving a person, and losing that love can hurt every bit as much. Sometimes, we lose a love in ways that have nothing to with dying—people change, circumstances change. Hurts can't be healed and people go their separate ways. But animals don't break up with us and move on; they die and leave us forever, never having hurt us, never moving on to another love, never betraying us. Maybe that is why it's so hard to let them go and why the hurt from losing them runs so deep. To have never been let down by the one you love makes losing them all the more heartbreaking.

I wish dogs lived longer, but I suppose it would be twice as hard to let them go if they did. Fifteen years is a long time. Part of what makes life worth living are the relationships we forge as we live it, and relationships with animals are every bit as important as those with other humans; different, less complex, and shorter, but just as satisfying.

Some people lose their way and prefer to spend time with their animal friends rather than humans. The temptation to do so is understandable; pets seldom let us down, and when they do, it's usually because we let them down first. If we don't let them out, they pee in the house. If we don't give them proper exercise, they find a way to get their own and the result can be costly. If they just refuse to listen, it is because we have failed to properly communicate with them. It is in a dog's nature to make us happy; in fact, it is their number-one priority. What's not to like?

Chapter 12

THE SPARK

Wilson was safely tucked away in the air-conditioned comfort of the Alpha Dog Transport trailer, along with a few dozen other homeless dogs, all headed for an uncertain future. We knew that great things were in store for Wilson, but he had no way of knowing what was happening; only that things had changed. Again.

His life had been rife with changes until this point; we know that he was born in Arkansas, in all probability in a puppy mill. The Internet is full of places that look fabulous on a computer screen and come with lovely stories of rolling hills and freshwater streams and puppies running through tall grass, lovingly followed by their doting parents, all under the watchful eye of a responsible breeder.

Those places may well exist, but what definitely does exist is the anti-heaven so vastly different than the delightful world described by web designers. The reality is stark contrast to what we are shown—dark, excruciatingly hot trailers in the woods filled with animals who breed until they die or can no longer provide a revenue stream for the people who own them. Conditions at these places are appalling while malnourished mothers give birth to malnourished pups. Four weeks later, those pups are taken away from their moms, packed in crates, and shipped off to unsuspecting buyers. The mom is put right back at it and is impregnated as soon as possible; if she barks, metal rods are shoved down her throat to sever her vocal cords. She lies in her own excrement and eats the floor sweepings from dog food companies—companies that ship their waste in boxcars to people who buy it in bulk and feed it to their charges, not for nourishment, but to keep them alive long enough to deliver another pile of cash.

When the dogs have finished being productive, some are shot in the head or clubbed to death and their body thrown in a fire. One of the mother's pups takes over pumping out four-legged money producers, and the cycle repeats itself.

Ol' Wilson and his sister were born, then sold to a pet store, bought, and then lived with a lady and her kids. He didn't like living there much and took every chance he had to escape. He would run wild, and I'm sure he had loads of fun, until he got hungry, or cold, or afraid of the bigger, wild animals that shared his roaming grounds. Then, the life of a vagabond, freedom-loving little dog got much more complicated, and being on his own was not nearly as much fun as anticipated, so he would slink back to the only home he knew. He would then be punished, reprimanded, probably whacked, and made to feel like a bad, bad boy.

Cheri took a liking to Wilson after seeing him running free with his sister too often. She had a feeling about him and knew that he was special. And he is.

All living things need to be nurtured. People, animals, plants, even bugs need some sort of interaction with other beings to thrive. Flowers need bees, bees need flowers, bugs need something to do, and other bugs to do it with. People need other people to take care of them, to love them, to feed them and educate them, and lead them toward their inherent tendency toward good. Left to fend for ourselves, we would revert back to a single-minded cell that does whatever it takes to survive. A dog is no different. The survival instinct will take over if prodded, and he will never know what he could have been if given a chance.

All too often, a child's creative spark never gets a chance to blossom for the simple yet cruel reason that nobody notices it. That creative fire burns brightly for a few years and, if stoked, grows. With the proper guidance, it is brought under control. The gift is then nurtured, and the child is given the chance to be everything he or she is supposed to be.

Or not. Far too often, potential for greatness is overlooked, and before long even the child forgets just how great he or she is and settles for existing rather than living.

Much is the same for dogs. Wilson was headed for a life of being "trouble." His free spirit was nearly extinguished because nobody saw that special something in him until Cheri came along. She knew deep down that this dog needed a chance. He simply had to be given the love he needed to thrive and grow, and be loved as much as his little heart could handle so that the love inside of him could be expressed and given freely to anybody who asked for it. Or needed it.

Chapter 13

CONTRACTS

Mr. Wilson was neutered at the Womack Animal Hospital in Arkansas. FOHARI paid the bill. He also had a haircut and bath, was vaccinated, tested for heartworm, treated for tics and fleas, and given every shot necessary to keep a puppy healthy. Before FOHARI agreed to let us adopt him, we had to sign a contract.

It was a pretty straightforward legal document designed to protect the adopted pets and FOHARI. By signing, we agreed to keep the dog as an indoor pet and supply identification tags he would wear at all times. They wanted to make sure we kept him on a leash and brought him to the vet regularly. One of the contract provisions I found particularly reassuring was that FOHARI required we return the dog to them if we found that we could not properly care for him. Other than that, the rest of the document basically released FOHARI from responsibility should the dog go buggy and cause harm to another person, place, or thing. Seemed reasonable enough to us. We signed the contract, had it signed by witnesses, paid the donation, and got ready to accept Mr. Wilson into our home.

These folks were not kidding around when it came to animal welfare. In addition to signing the necessary forms and making the suggested donation, a volunteer from FOHA visited our home and, after looking around for a while, determined that we were fit pet owners. They then checked our references and actually called our veterinarian, Dr. Glenn Brewer from Airport Animal Hospital, and Cheryl's friend Maria. Both gave us glowing reviews.

Wilson had no idea any of these things happened before he was united with us. For all he knew, the whole thing was predestined and everything was going according to plan. For all I knew, he could've been right.

Organizations like FOHA depend almost exclusively on donations and volunteers to stay afloat. Running a pet rescue outfit is no small undertaking, and countless hours are spent making sure things are done right. Cheryl thought the time was right for us to get a dog, and FOHA made it happen. We got exactly what we wanted, and what we wanted was all we could handle at this moment of our lives. I would have loved to give a bigger dog a home, give a pit bull another chance, but our home situation simply doesn't allow for the time needed to take care of such a dog properly.

Just because we wanted to adopt a dog did not mean the dog would automatically appear. FOHA's goal, like all legitimate pet rescue outfits, is to find a homeless pet a place to live. For good. Taking an animal in does not equate to giving an animal a home. What good would it be for the animal to leave a bad situation and enter one that is worse? Or to be cast aside when the novelty wears off, dumped at the shelter, or abandoned by the side of the road?

There is a reason for all of the work, paperwork, inspections, and financial commitment; the pet needs a place to call home.

Wilson was on his way from Arkansas, and he was headed exactly where he was meant to be: living with us in a little house in Rhode Island, working his magic and touching every person he meets.

Chapter 14

THEY'RE HERE

"They're here!" said Cheryl, her anticipation and excitement barely contained. A big rig pulling a small trailer appeared on the access road near the highway and turned into the rest area. It drove past us and headed for the far corner of the lot. The people waiting gravitated toward the truck, forming a line as close to it as they could. There was no shoving or pushing, no Black Friday madness. Rather, an orderly line developed and the folks who were first in line made it there by chance, just happening to be in the right place at the right time. As it turned out, the last in line was the best spot of them all. Watching families meet their adopted pets was the best show I had ever seen, better than the movies, the World Series, and the Super Bowl combined.

We watched the crowd assemble, then drove our car close to the gang, got out, and watched from about a hundred feet away. The truck's shadow cast a covering of shade on the new dog owners;

a gesture of kindness that I first thought was random until I met the people driving the truck. Kindness is not a random occurrence for the people who operate Alpha Dog Transport; it is deeply embedded in their DNA.

Two men got out of the cab and sauntered toward the trailer, smiling briefly at the folks who had gathered before disappearing inside. We waited, some of us not knowing quite what to expect, others knowing exactly what was coming, because they had done it before.

Our new friends had been through a lot, the most recent being a four-day highway road trip. Dogs live in the moment and, as far as I know, are unable to worry about the future. I imagine they are aware of the varying emotions that different moments bring and in all likelihood know when things are dull. They understand *what is*, and the what is that had been going on for days must have been an eternity to the dogs. For me, knowing a destination waits at the end of a long journey makes the tedium bearable; being in the limbo of perpetual motion must have been difficult for them, as the miles and hours added up, the frequent stops to pee, eat, and stretch the only breaks in the monotony.

The first people in line were the first to be introduced to their new pet. If those people were anything like me and Cheryl, they had seen the pictures, read the description of their new friends, researched the breeds, knew kind of what to expect, yet were still anxious over what waited for them. Adopting a homeless pet is a risky venture—especially a pet that had been transported more than a thousand miles to find a home.

"Michael, look at him!" Cheryl exclaimed. One of the people from the transport company had opened a side door of the trailer, the one nearest the cab, and stepped out, holding the first adoptee.

This dog wasn't at all what I expected. I had envisioned a scared little rascal; timid, shy, and unwilling to socialize. Instead, a bundle of energy and love appeared and was handed off to his new owners. They let him onto the ground, and he circled his new owners, sniffed and sniffed some more, then graciously let his new mom pick him up and hold him in her arms. The woman was overwhelmed with joy, and tears streamed down her face as she walked past us, holding the brown, mixed Labrador . . . hound dog . . . terrier thing so tightly, I thought he might be crushed.

But he wasn't crushed, not even close. He was as overjoyed as she was, and when he licked her face she didn't mind. The lady's husband followed, a smile on his face that appeared as soon as he saw his new friend come out of the truck, and grew wider as he saw the effect his new friend had on his wife. It was a look of pure joy—true, uncomplicated, uninterrupted by phones or TVs or Internets—just a middle-aged man and his dog and his wife, who was beyond happy. They left, the three of them, lost in their new world, which would revolve around their pet, who had traveled so far to be with them.

"This is incredible," I said to Cheryl as the man from the truck company went inside to get another one. She smiled then—a true, soulful smile that transcended time and place—and caught me. I smiled, too, and didn't stop for hours.

We leaned on the hood of our car, not wanting to rush things, content for once to stand back and let what was happening happen. It was enough just to live in the moment and share that moment with a group of people who, for a little while anyway, forgot about their busy lives and focused on the miracle that was happening right now.

Chapter 15

FOSTERING

Wilson had lived with Cheri as a foster dog for about a month before Cheryl saw his picture on the Internet. After speaking with her about Wilson and the life he lived prior to being rescued, I was still expecting the dog to be a little weird—although, hearing her description of him, how he was, and how he acted with her did help to alleviate some of our fears.

Our daughter Danielle had told us that her friend Sue would be at the rest stop to pick up Buttons and Dingo, two dogs who had traveled with Wilson and would be staying at Sue's home until permanent homes for them could be found. Sue and her daughter, Cassie, waited with us, and watched as more dogs were brought from the trailer and into the arms of their adoptive parents or their new foster parents.

"Have you fostered animals before this?" Cheryl asked Sue as we settled in and watched the people getting acquainted with their new dogs.

"These are my first," said Sue. "My husband thinks I'm nuts."

I thought she might be kind of nuts, as well. My experience with dogs is that they tend to grow on you, and getting to know them happens fast—and bonding with them even faster. Even the strange ones find a way to charm people in their own special way. There is something about the species that makes them instantly part of you, and there is not much we can do to stop the emotional bonding once it starts. I would have had a hard time giving up a dog once he'd lived with me for even a brief amount of time. I had to give Sue and Cassie credit; they were stronger people than me when it came to kindness to animals. I do love animals, and take good care of them, but mine is more of a selfish kindness—I get back far more than I give.

The next people in line were a family of four—a mom and dad, son and daughter. The kids were eight and ten years old, the girl older than the boy. They waited; mom and dad patiently, the boy and girl not so much, until Jeff appeared at the doorway of the trailer, holding their new dog in his arms. Jeff handed her over to the dad, who instantly melted, and his kids crowded around him reaching up to touch her. His wife watched and smiled. The smiles that appeared on the faces of the people at Exit 89 off of Route 395 lit up that dreary rest stop, turning it into the most joyous place on Earth. I have never seen such a display of spontaneous happiness coming from so many different people. A young couple took the family's place at the front of the line as the dad stepped away from the truck and let his family's new protector down. The young yellow Labrador mix mingled with her new family, her tail slowly gaining life, creeping from between her legs. Then it was free, and it went back and forth slowly at first but picked up speed as the boy petted her head, and the girl rubbed her back, and the mom stroked her head, right between the ears, which turned the tail into a blur.

The young couple's new dog appeared in the doorway, and Jeff walked him down the steps as Kevin handled the paperwork. Jeff gave this one to the guy as his girlfriend recorded every second on her iPhone. Normally, people who choose to take pictures of every memorable event in their lives rather than simply enjoying the moment annoy me, but these two made me smile, and I was a little envious that our flip phones from another era would not do justice for the greeting that awaited us. Enjoying the moment is great, but having a few pictures to tweak the memory a few years down the road makes it even better.

The young family that had adopted their dog was off to our right, walking their dog before putting her into their car for the ride home. They couldn't get enough of her, or she them. Behind us was a guardrail that protected people from driving down an embankment, and a little grassy knoll between it and the drop-off made for an inviting place for the newly freed dogs to lead their new masters. They wiggled under, or simply walked under the rail, and watered the grass before taking their place in whichever car they were led to, all ready for the last leg of their journeys home.

Another came out of the trailer, and another, and yet another. The line that had formed was slowly diminishing, but many people lingered after greeting their pets, perhaps captured by the magic that had been created by our presence at the rest stop. We all were part of something special, something we would cherish and remember always.

For Jeff and Kevin, this was the culmination of a long arduous journey that had begun on Wednesday and still had another long highway trek before finishing. I could tell they were in no hurry to end things though, and they took their time introducing each and every one of us to our dogs. The goodwill was contagious, and a bond formed, unspoken but so strong you could almost see it form between us—one of those miracles that happen so seldom during our time on Earth, when everything is just as it should be, and the predominant feeling in the air is simply happiness to be alive.

Chapter 16

KIP

"I think that's Kip," said Cheryl as we watched Jeff hand a little foxy-looking Pomeranian over to a woman who immediately held the little guy close and rubbed his back for a moment before letting him down.

"Is he the one that can't eat?" I asked.

"He can only eat soft food."

"Forever?"

"I think so, poor thing. He's going to need a lot of care."

The people at FOHARI had compiled and distributed a list of the dogs to be delivered to the rest stop, and on the list was a brief description of the dog and his or her history. We had read the list a few times while waiting for Sunday to come and remembered Kip's story.

We watched poor ol' Kip hit the ground, his face a little deformed but not too bad. The damage to his jaw was on the inside mostly, the result of a swift kick from somebody who didn't expect their little dog to bark. The second his paws hit the ground, he bounced up and tried to get back into the arms of the woman he had just met. He jumped and circled and actually smiled a giant deformed grin when she reached down and lifted him from the ground and back into her arms. He licked, and squirmed, and licked some more, then squirmed some more. She let him back on the ground and he ran around in circles and led her to the promised land, the grassy knoll where he relieved himself, then decided to do some exploring, the joy in his heart expressed with every energetic step. His foster mom followed on the end of her leash, astonished by the resiliency displayed by this ten-pound dynamo whose spirit could not be extinguished by an abusive owner.

Kip led his human away from the crowd, and they walked toward her car and drove away.

Some people do not deserve to be in the company of such heroic, gentle, and loving companions. Something is missing from these people's souls, and they simply cannot see or feel the special bond that can exist between humans and animals if we allow them space in our hearts.

"Do you hear that?" I asked Cheryl.

"What?"

"The dogs. They're not barking. It's quiet in there, everybody is behaving."

"This is unbelievable," she said, and we took it all in.

It certainly was.

Chapter 17

PAWS

A guy about my age was next in line. He was rugged, dressed in jeans and a red flannel shirt. He didn't seem to be the type to rescue homeless dogs. When Jeff appeared with a brown, hairy, mixed-breed thing, and Kevin handed over the manila envelope with the dog's medical records and as much history as they could find, I saw a different person altogether. He was one of us, and the look of exultation on his face was priceless. He walked away from the crowd, just him and his dog, looking into his new puppy's eyes, getting his face licked, hypnotized by the living creature in his arms that gave unconditionally to a person who he had never met. A bond was instantly established between the two, one that would last the entire length of the dog's life.

One of the people who fostered dogs was next, identified by her jacket emblazoned with giant letters, PAWS, on the back.

"What's PAWS mean?" I asked Cheryl, assuming that she would know. After all, she did find out about all this. Had it not been for her, exit 89 off of 395 would have been just one of the million and one places I have never been.

"People helping animals. They hook people up with abandoned dogs and cats."

"Yeah, but what's PAWS stand for?"

"I just told you, people helping animals."

"That would be PHA."

"You can't say PHA. Nobody would remember it."

"So what's PAWS stand for?"

"Does it matter?"

"I guess not . . . I just wish I knew."

"Google it."

"I don't have a Googler with me."

"What's a Googler?"

"It's a thing that lets you Google stuff."

"Like an iPhone?"

"Yeah, exactly! So what does PAWS stand for?"

"I told you, People Helping Animals."

"That would be PHA."

"Forget it."

"Okay, it's not that important."

There's nothing like meaningful conversation on a beautiful day.

The dog that the lady from PAWS took from Jeff and Kevin was older, maybe seven years old. She was terrified, and her tail was between her legs, and her ears were flat on her head, and she refused to make eye contact with anybody. She just tried to melt into the pavement. She simply did not want to be noticed; being invisible was much safer than being seen. She hid behind her foster mother's legs, and the mom's assistant, also wearing a PAWS jacket, knelt next to the abused dog and then sat on the ground and held her in her arms. I was mesmerized, unable to tear my damp eyes away from the drama that was happening so close to me. I could smell the scent of fear coming from the dog.

"Pets are worth saving."

"They sure are," I said, watching as the two women showered the poor dog with patience and affection.

"That's what PAWS means."

It took me a minute, but eventually it all became clear.

PAWS means a lot of things to a lot of different people. There are numerous organizations named PAWS, and most exist for the sole reason of helping animals. It doesn't really matter what each organization's letters stand for; what matters is that there are people who volunteer their time helping those who have no voice.

For me, PAWS means "people are worthy souls."

Chapter 18

HANDOVER

The line, once longer than the truck, had dwindled to just a few people, and we made our way closer. Sue and Cassie had just met their foster dogs and were busy getting acquainted. That left me and Cheryl.

"Go ahead," she said to me when Jeff went back into the trailer to get our dog.

"No, you," I said, even though I knew it would have to be me. I'd be the first of us to hold him, even though she and I both had wanted it to be her. It isn't fair, not fair at all, but when you have multiple sclerosis, and simply standing takes every ounce of energy you can muster, sacrifices must be made. The decision had already been made, and not by us. Nature and circumstance sometimes dictate the flow of things. We have learned to accept things as they are, not how we want them to be.

Jeff appeared, and in his arms was Wilson. I had been looking forward to this moment all morning, and here it was. I hesitated, then reached out and took him. Jeff was all smiles, I was all smiles, Kevin and Cheryl were all smiles, and even Wilson smiled. I thought he would be too tired to do much, but he simply could not wait to start loving his new masters. He squirmed a little, but then relaxed, and his tiny tongue snaked out and he licked my hand. He snuggled into my arms and rested, looking up at me from the cradle I had created, and those eyes of his worked their magic. He had me. I simply could not look away from him. It was as if he were born right there in my arms, belonged there, and would be happy to spend the rest of his life just laying there, every now and then bestowing one of his looks my way with a snaky little lick between naps. It would be a good life, and I was willing to allow it.

He eventually decided to get down and check things out. Cheryl was near, and to her he sauntered, stretching a little, yawning a little, and licking a lot.

A chorus of "Oh my god, he's so cute!" erupted, followed by the obligatory "Can I hold him?" which lasted a few minutes, but before long it was just Cheryl, Wilson, and me, sitting in our car, looking out at the emptying parking lot where so much joy had happened. A transport truck of a different kind came into focus, just one-hundred feet from where the greetings had taken place. It was a car carrier; chock full of brand-new Audis. There was a time when a brand-new Audi would have been overwhelming, and nothing could have stopped me from getting closer to it, touching it, dreaming of driving it, or at the very least sitting in it. Here was a truckload of them and I couldn't have cared less. Funny how things change as life goes on and different circumstances dictate what matters; dreams change along with those needs and become more appropriate. Those big dreams about fancy cars and lavish vacations just don't mean much anymore, and seldom do I think about them. When I do, it's with a chuckle, and I wonder where my life would have led had I obtained the material possessions I once thought were imperative. Knowing that what is essential in life is actually invisible to the eye is knowledge gained from living; you eventually find that in getting the things you thought you wanted, the wanting is often better than the getting.

Now, the other transport truck—the one that had brought Wilson to us—was the one that mattered. It had taken me a while to even notice the millions of dollars' worth of automobiles, and I had been standing a few feet away moments ago. Jeff and Kevin were joined by Kelly, Jeff's wife, and Sir who had been sitting patiently in the cab while all the excitement happened just outside his door. Kevin went back inside the trailer, and I got out of the car to introduce myself to Jeff and his wife and thank them for bringing Wilson to us.

I shook Jeff's hand, and he was appreciative of my thank-you, but seemed awfully tired and much more interested in Kelly, who he spoke to softly before giving her a big kiss. He walked back to the truck and got ready for the last leg of his journey, which included more dogs, another rest stop, and dozens of eager people waiting for their new dogs. Had I not had Wilson and Cheryl waiting for me in the car, I might have thought Jeff was the luckiest man on Earth, bringing joy to the masses with a pretty wife, who worked with him and obviously loved him, and a loyal dog by his side. But I had Cheryl, and now Wilson, and luck is what you make of what you have. At the moment, I had a car full of good luck and couldn't wait to enjoy it.

Chapter 19

IMPRINTS

We were the last to leave the lot; everybody else had their dog or dogs and were already headed home. Jeff, Kevin, and Sir were on their way to Maine with the last of their deliveries. Kelly was gone, and the only ones left were the truckload of Audis, Cheryl, Wilson, and me. We had bought a bed for the little guy during our tri-county doggie supply tour and it had come with a little red teddy bear and a comfy red blanket. Cheryl wrapped Wilson in that and put the teddy bear and Wilson on her lap. I put the car in drive and we left. The place where so much happiness had just occurred returned to what it is without the participation of mankind: a lifeless lot.

Is it truly lifeless, though?

Do places retain the emotion that permeates the space, and then leaves? Do good experiences leave an indelible imprint into the space where the happiness occurred, and will the aftereffects linger? Houses can be haunted—I think so, anyway—why not parking lots? I think the lot just past Exit 89 off of Route 395 in Connecticut is one of those magical places, not because it just is, but because of all the good things that happen there. Ours is just one day of many, and every week different people come to pick up their rescued pets. Of course, there are repeat visitors— the animal rescue organization representatives and foster families come to the lot over and over—but they are also joined by the one-time-only visitors. Those once-only visitors had best beware, because something happens in these places, and they often find themselves coming back, again and again, either to foster or to adopt another homeless pet or to accompany a friend who will join the ranks.

Cheryl sat in the passenger seat, her eyes locked on Wilson's, and the two started a connection that would grow until they became inseparable. All the energy he had shown earlier was gone, and he relaxed in my wife's arms and tried to stay awake, perhaps afraid that what seemed so safe and good would be taken away and he would be cast aside again. His big brown eyes fluttered, closed and opened, then closed again.

"I love him," said Cheryl, holding onto the living, breathing package on her lap.

"He's tired," I said. And we drove in comfortable silence toward home, feeling the road as we sped over small hills and shallow valleys. Moving while being held was a welcome experience for Wilson; four days of traveling in a trailer had taken its toll on his spirit, and he relaxed completely during the hour ride.

"Let's show Brittany," said Cheryl as we neared our exit. Our daughter Brittany lives a few minutes off the highway and was home when I called.

"Hey Brittany, want to see the cutest thing in the world?" I asked.

"Uh, sure," she said, never knowing quite what to expect when I call.

"We'll be there in five minutes."

She knew we were getting a dog but probably was not aware that today was the day. She worries about us and was thrilled when we told her we were going to adopt a pet. She and her husband, Eric, had been considering adding a dog to their new family, which consists of Brittany, Eric, and Mr. Sox, a giant tuxedo-wearing cat who ran their home.

Cheryl stayed in the car, holding Wilson while he slept, and I went to the door and got Brittany and brought her outside to the car.

"Oh my God!" Brittany said when she saw him, which woke him. She reached for him and lifted him from her mother's arms. He licked her nose and a friendship was born. She let him down and his energy rebounded. He jumped and ran around in circles for a while before resting again, this time letting Brittany hold him until he fell asleep.

We stayed for a while, and Eric came home with some groceries.

"Who is that?" he asked when he saw him.

"This is Wilson," said Cheryl, who had taken him back from her daughter. She looked at him and instinctively added, "Mr. Wilson."

He opened his eyes, and the long schnauzer eyebrows crossed a little. He tilted his head to the side, his furry face showing the prominent moustache indicative of the Schnauzer breed that made up half his pedigree. Then he fell back to sleep, wrapped in the red blanket and held by his new mother, whom he had already grown attached to.

Mr. Wilson had arrived.

We drove away, and I thought how fortunate I was to have a family with whom I could share everything. Danielle and Brittany had moved on and out of our home, but no matter in which city they made their homes, they will always live under our roof. From the moment I entered their lives, it could be no other way. I like to think the three great loves of my life came all at once, and no matter what may come, we will always have a connection that I had never imagined possible.

That they were five and seven when I became part of their lives is irrelevant to us. We share a love that is every bit as solid as one created by conception. Some poor fool once mentioned to Cheryl that I would never know the powerful love that comes from having a child of my own. But Cheryl knew, and the girls knew, and I knew just how wrong that person's opinion was. Somebody who has never felt what we feel can never know, for we have the luxury of knowing through experience exactly how deeply a man's love is capable of running, and we know that my love for my wife and the girls runs as deep as it gets.

I do not know how it feels to hold my own newborn infant fresh from the womb and to feel the connection between man and woman embodied in the life they created. I do know how it feels to be accepted by a five-year-old child whose "real" father turned out to be not so great. After a period of uncertainty and getting to know each other, I knew how it how it felt to have her arms wrapped around my neck as I picked her injured body off the grass after she fell from our tree house. She held me close and I comforted her while we waited for her tears to slow. Then they stopped, and her smile returned, and I knew that she felt safe with me, and loved, and that, through me, everything was going to be okay. Being accepted by choice rather than by right of birth is as good as it gets.

I wouldn't trade that feeling for a thousand newborns.

Chapter 20

THE RESCUE DOG

We needed food; it was the one thing we neglected to buy during our pet supply shopping spree. So we said goodbye to Brittany and Eric and went home, stopping on the way to pick up a bag of dry food and a few cans of beef and chicken, specially formulated for small dogs, of course.

We are fortunate in having a holistic pet supply store nearby. All About Pets is owned and operated by Denise, on whom we have learned to depend for all our pets' nutritional well-being. It just made sense to us to feed our little crew the best possible food, and Denise always carries it. Better than that, she advises us on what is best and why. It costs a little more up front, but in the long run is well worth the investment. We have fed our pets a grain-free diet long before it became fashionable to do so. A diet lower in carbohydrates is closer to what a dog's metabolism and digestive system needs. All dogs are descendants of wolves and, having taken care of a wolf-dog for twelve years, we saw the advantages of a grain-free diet shortly after starting it. My favorite result? Fewer carbohydrates in the diet equates to less stool from the dog. And the density makes for an easy pick-up. The higher quality food, the higher quality stool, and high-quality stool means a higher quality of life for the person delegated to picking up the aforementioned stool. In addition to making my life easier, the grain-free diet is linked to a decrease in overweight and obese dogs. Allergies are common in our pets, and the culprit is often the grains we feed them. Research has shown the grain itself is not the problem, but rather the pesticides used while growing the grain.

"Hey Denise, look at this!" I said when I entered the store, pointing out the window at Wilson and Cheryl.

"You got a dog," she said, looking completely unimpressed, but I knew her better than that. She is one of those super cool people who never gets rattled or overly excited, but always is amused by what goes on around her.

"Sure did, just picked him up at a rest stop on 395." I couldn't wait to tell her our story. Owen, her pug, raced up to me and gave me the obligatory sniff before going back to work, which, judging from his guilty demeanor, had more to do with sabotaging dog food bags than guarding the store. Isaac, her big Akita, stayed in his crate behind the counter, looked up, then went back to sleep. It must be cool owning a pet store, I thought, and bringing your dogs to work with you where they fit right in.

"Don't tell me, let me guess—he's a rescue dog," said Denise, a funny little grin on her face.

"As a matter of fact, he is," I said. "How did you guess?"

"Oh, I don't know," she replied, "must be because he looks like he was abused."

"How did you know that?"

"Didn't you know?" She answered in her whimsically sarcastic way. "The Rescue Dog is the fastest growing breed in the world right now. Everybody wants one and they're all, 'abused.'" She made little finger quotation marks when she said *abused*, and I couldn't help but chuckle. People see things differently, and Denise sees a lot more of the inner workings of the pet supply-and-demand world than I do.

"Well," I began, unwilling to let go of the awesomeness that is me by adopting an abused Rescue Dog. "They found Wilson chained to an old coal stove, feeble and starving, rib bones sticking out of his body, icicles stuck to his face, and nothing but rat bones to chew on for weeks."

"See, I told you he was abused." She smiled and peeked out of the store window at our car, which we had parked in front of her door. Mr. Wilson slept peacefully on his mother's lap.

"Well he really was."

"I don't doubt it for a minute," she said, and stepped outside to say hello to Cheryl and to meet Mr. Wilson.

It's funny how people's experiences slant their views toward the world we inhabit. I readily grasped the concept that all dogs from "the south" were abused and needed rescue. I never questioned the validity of the reported puppy mills. I had YouTube to affirm my suspicions, and the countless American Society for the Prevention of Cruelty to Animals clips to prove I was right. Not only that, but Sarah McLachlan's lovely song, "Angel," haunts me every time I hear it, in large part due to the song being played over images of suffering puppies and kitties, compliments of the ASPCA. And if I can't trust Sarah McLachlan, then who can I trust?

New breed of dog, "the Abused Rescue Dog." Ha! I had to admit, though, she got me thinking, and when I get thinking I go straight to Google and let Google do the thinking for me.

It didn't take long for me to become completely confused; on one hand, the ASPCA is the greatest animal rescue outfit in the history of the world. On the other, they are a bunch of stuffed suits who use every nickel but one that was donated to the abandoned and abused animals to give themselves outrageous salaries and lavish vacations. Somebody even said Sarah gets paid to do their songs! According to Sarah, from her appearance on VH1's *Storytellers* the song was written for Jonathan Melvoin, the keyboardist for Smashing Pumpkins who overdosed on heroin and died in 1996. Her role as a spokesperson for the ASPCA and their use of the song has helped raise millions of dollars for the organization and subsequently has helped countless dogs and cats. It is a great song that elicits raw emotion from most people who hear it, and I don't need Google to tell me that the value of that song far exceeds any amount of money the artist responsible for it earns.

I like believing in things and trusting people and organizations. The world of Google is one big contradiction, and if I want to believe that people mean what they say and say what they mean, then that is just the way it is going to have to be. Mr. Wilson is a Rescue Dog and was abused and born in a puppy mill until proven otherwise!

Denise's take on things and her experience is far different from mine. She is in the retail pet-supply business, and if my experiences as a firefighter/EMT are any indication, things are not always what they seem. I do know that she is dedicated to the health and welfare of the animals she is responsible for, both her own and those of the people who trust her and heed her advice. Denise is by no means extreme in her opinions and experience, but offers a needed perspective from a different point of view.

But I need balance. I tend to tune out if I hear too much on a given subject or if all I hear is one side of the topic. Society needs extremes. Organizations like People for the Ethical Treatment of Animals are passionate about their cause, and their dedication to what they believe is an inspiration. They manage to stay in the news and on people's minds and hopefully that translates into an improved environment for all living things.

Balance exists, and perhaps someday I will find it and learn the truth. Until then, I can only do what I think is right, and make my little place in the world the best, most ethical place I can. By supporting the ASPCA and, to some degree, the philosophy of PETA, my corner of the world is doing just fine, thank you very much!

The dogs that I've been responsible for during my life never had the option of shopping for their dinner. They did occasionally hunt for it, but their skills had waned considerably from their ancestral days. Mr. Wilson deserves a good diet, one without pesticides and one that will keep him allergy-free and healthy. Denise supplies what we need, with a good dose of reality to boot!

The information age has its ups and downs. If not for the Internet and search engines, we would never have found our dog. Alas, we also would never have known that every fact ever known by man is suspect. If necessary, Google can help me diagnose a pimple on my buttocks as terminal cancer or a persistent cough as tuberculosis. It could also teach me that I could discourage skunks from nesting under my shed by peeing around its perimeter every night and, one minute later, it can convince me that what traditions I thought were from my Irish heritage are actually African-based.

But Mr. Wilson wasn't complaining about me finding him on the Internet, so neither would I.

There was something special going on, something none of us had imagined possible. Wilson, or rather Mr. Wilson, had arrived, and instead of being a chore or a burden, he instantly became a blessing in our lives. Without even thinking about how or why, he was already a permanent part of our family. Immediately, we knew that he wasn't just "our dog." He was one of us and would be for as long as he lived. It was up to us to make sure that his time with us would be the best time possible, and doing so meant feeding him well and teaching him how to behave while retaining his personality. The feeding part would be easy, but training would be hard, we knew; that cute little face begged anybody who gazed upon it to heed his every whim and desire, be it eating furniture, peeing on the rug, digging a new garden, or jumping up on anybody who came close. But he deserved to be taught the ways of the world and his place in it.

One of the books we read explained the pack hierarchy in vivid detail. Mr. Wilson had to be made aware of his place in the home. He was a valuable asset to our family, but was not the center of our universe. He needed to be shown that we were in charge and made the rules. It was absolutely imperative that the pecking order be established right away.

We got home, settled in, and decided we could start all of that the following day.

PART II: THE PAST

Chapter 21

WALKING

I do my best thinking while walking. Since we lost Zimba and Lakota a few years back, I haven't been walking all that much. Since Cheryl's legs turned to noodles, I've walked even less. Now and then I do go for an extended stroll, most of the time to work out at a gym that's a mile and a half from my house. It's a nice walk; when it's cold out I do it in about fifteen minutes, when it's hot, twenty. I like to lift weights and used to be able to lift lots of them all at once. Now, it's all about the reps. The middle-aged man's brain sometimes forgets that his body is not what it once was, and nothing is a better reminder than lying on a bench being crushed by a barbell with two forty-fives on each side in a gym full of people. It is rather humbling to squeak out a cry for help with 225 pounds squeezing your chest. Lifting light weights and doing lots of reps is a good way to stay somewhat fit as we age and not get hurt in the process. It doesn't make me a lightweight, just a smarter weightlifter.

The place I go to is a no-judgment gym; we cannot comment on the physique of our counterpart gym rats because there, everybody looks great. We have complimentary bagels in the morning, with cream cheese on the side, and pizza on Tuesday nights. Every now and then a voice comes over the loudspeaker and tells everybody to grab a Tootsie Roll on the way out, because "you earned it!" Grunting is strictly prohibited and, if a grunt escapes, a loud siren fills the place and the grunter is given a warning. Three warnings and you're out! Working hard is also prohibited, and nobody ever changes, we all stay the same.

My new gym is a far cry from the places I used to go, where people would push themselves to the extreme, getting stronger, lifting more, looking great, and getting better. Cheryl and I were members of Gold's Gym in Warwick, Rhode Island, for years and were part of the culture. Six days a week, fifty-two weeks a year, we were there, and we loved every minute of it. Cheryl could bench press a car, I could lift a building on my back, and we both could run for miles. And we didn't eat Tootsie Rolls, bagels, or pizza, at least not at the gym. But even the best bodies don't last forever, and strength ebbs as years progress. I'm older now, and the "workout facility" is close, and it's only ten bucks a month and within walking distance. But best of all, I think I'm in better shape than most of the people there, but I'm not judging.

In the opposite direction from the gym is a pretty little beach and, when the idea of lifting not-so-heavy things over and over doesn't thrill me, I find my path leading in the direction of the sea. It is a much more pleasant walk, and the destination far more appealing. Nicely kept homes line the streets that lead to the beach; the yards get smaller as the water draws closer. Most places you will find the yards and homes increase in size the closer you get to the shore, as the affluent fill the pricy waterfront properties, but not on the land that leads to Gaspee Point. A wealthy family owns the acreage and leases lots to people who build homes on the land. It is one of the few places in New England where a person of modest means can live on the water or near enough to walk to it.

Everybody in Rhode Island knows the American Revolution began at Gaspee Point on June 9, 1772. A British tax collecting schooner ran aground during low tide while chasing a smaller ship, the *Hannah*; the captain was apparently not aware that a sandbar from the point extended well into Narragansett Bay and, while stuck in the sand, some Revolutionary War–era merchants boarded longboats and paddled up the bay from Providence to Warwick, captured the crew, and set the schooner on fire. Mind you, Revolutionary War–era merchants were not at all like the merchants of today. Back then, the merchants were often rabble-rousers and tended to be wealthy businessmen who had the most to lose by engaging in illegal acts against the crown. Things like their lives, livelihood, and sacred honor were at stake. The men who burned the Gaspee were led by the Sons of Liberty, and a man named John Brown was one of the leaders of the expedition. The owners of the land that I walk when I visit the beach are descendents of the very same man.

I love living in a place with constant reminders of years and events long past. The past fascinates me, and I truly believe that he who does not learn from it is condemned to repeat it. Knowing that a place so rich with historical significance is within walking distance from my home gives me a great excuse to avoid the gym and stay off of the treadmill and distractions from the cable TV that goes with it.

The neighborhood streets lead to a partially hidden gate in a four-foot-high chain-link fence. A path behind the gate straddles two properties. In Rhode Island, laws exist near the waterfront, ensuring the public's right to access the shore, so there are no worries of trespassing. Somebody used railroad ties and a lot of hard work to make a stairway from the street to the beach, and the thirty-foot descent and concentration and energy needed to safely navigate the steps provides a moment of clear thought and simple movement. Those moments empty the mind of its incessant chatter, erasing the needs and wants of life in civilization and preparing it for the serenity of the beach.

It was a great place to begin a revolution, and it is just as great a place to bring a dog. Very seldom is the beach occupied, and when it is, the half-mile expanse offers plenty of room to roam for the few people who dot the shoreline, most of whom are people walking their dogs.

It is one of the few remaining places in my town where a person can let their dogs run free and, when off the leash, Zimba and Lakota would do just that, straddling the water line and running away at breakneck speed, then turning around and running back to me. Of course, there would often be a foray into the tic-infested tall grass as well, but little in life comes without a price, even when you're a dog. Pulling the occasional tic from their dense fur was a small price to pay for the joy I felt watching them run unfettered by me.

One of my favorite things to do while at the beach with the dogs was to envision the schooner *Gaspée* stuck some fifty yards offshore, close enough for me to hit with a rock if it were still there, and picture the men from 1772 rowing toward it with an American Revolution ahead of them. They had no idea what the future would bring, or if their names and acts that night would be forever entwined in the history books, integral parts of a decade that set the course of history toward freedom, prosperity, and the pursuit of happiness, or if they would even survive the night.

I normally don't believe in spooks, but with so much history on the horizon, and the tides coming and going the same as they did in 1772, it's hard to not believe. There is something haunting about a lonely beach. After we had to put Zimba and Lakota down, I would walk alone through the quiet neighborhood, take the steps from civilization down to the shore, be left alone with my thoughts . . . and sometimes even the brightest day could grow dark.

Chapter 22

DAYDREAMING

I can see Providence from the beach, and I would often find myself daydreaming while looking at the city in the distance. I spent a large part of my adult life working there and witnessed more horrible things than I ever imagined possible. An ugly world exists in tandem with the one that I was familiar with. In that world, people are not spending their time adopting dogs, leading productive lives, and playing with the kids on the weekends. I wish I were not aware of that other world and had the luxury of seeing it only through the lens of the photographers when I read the paper or watched the news, but I do not. I lived it. I saw firsthand the carnage caused by greed, poverty, disillusionment, and despair. The things I saw are part of me forever, no matter how hard I try to forget.

At times, the memory of the bodies that we recovered from the docks would pop into my mind unbidden, and gloom embraced me. I could feel it coming, and all of the sun's brightness and positive thinking did nothing to stop its onslaught. It took over my mind and worked its way down my body, from my head to my toes, suffocating me. My breathing would quicken, and my heart would pound harder, so hard I could feel it knocking on my sternum. These days, the gloom comes and goes, and doesn't stay for as long as it once did, but I long for the day when it goes away for good.

The dead didn't bother me much the first few years of my career, but as the years progressed and the body count rose, I found it harder to shake the gloom that was brought to me as part of my job. People die. People kill themselves. They kill each other. They do it all the time. And when some poor soul finds the dying or the body, the first thing they do is call 911. That's where I would come in. It was my duty to make sure that the person who could be saved was so, or if it was too late, it was my job to make certain they were truly dead.

I did just that, often wondering the strangest things:

Did she know she was going to jump off the bridge when she put those earrings on?

Why did he get a tattoo the day before he hung himself?

Does it hurt to have a bullet fired into your brain?

Why did she have to wash up on shore in Providence?

Is there really life after death?

I've seen people my age lose interest in life and pull the plug on their difficulties. A firefighter in my city shot his ailing wife in the head, then turned the gun on himself, leaving notes to his children, explaining to them how they were better off and asking them to try and understand. I shudder to think of the suffering that comes to their boys when they drive past the home they were raised in—the place where their parents ended it all. Another couple made it to sixty when he decided that her debilitating illness had gone far enough, and his back pain was no longer bearable, and he ended it for the both of them, again leaving a note, this one saying, "no more suffering, no more pain, we're free now, pray for us."

I carry a lot with me on my walks. It was nice to have my dogs to share the load, and watching them alleviated the depression and allowed me to see a different side of life—a side that was simple and pure and full of the all-important trust and love that makes it worth living. But dogs don't live forever, and neither do people, but we do live longer than they do. Living longer means living more, seeing more, and absorbing more. The mind is like a sponge; it can only take so much before it spills over and can't take another drop.

People would often ask me, "How are you doing?" after some gruesome thing happened and made the news. I always answered the same way. "Fine."

Well, I wasn't fine. I just didn't like talking about the things I had seen. I thought it was disrespectful to the people who had been involved. I still think so.

But it may be necessary to describe just what happens when we go off to work. I learned long ago that writing can be therapeutic, so one day I put my fingers on the keyboard and rested them an hour later. The essay that resulted was published in the *Providence Journal,* then in a few EMS magazines, and eventually captured a worldwide audience. United States Senator Sheldon Whitehouse took the time to write me a note thanking me for my service after reading it.

That is all well and good, but one day a friend who had been experiencing difficulties with things that were "fine" told me about a place where police and firefighters could go to get help with post-traumatic stress disorder, depression, and other physiological problems that come with the job and are all too often ignored. She told me that my words were framed and placed in a prominent place in the organization's lobby. And that meant more to me than if the entire world had read the thing.

Twenty

Twenty years ago I thought I would do this job forever. I had a dream: work in Providence till I was 60 and they threw me out, and then move to somewhere where they have a volunteer fire department and put my experience to good use. The department offered a 50% pension after 20 years; we contribute 9.5% of our pay toward the fund, and the city contributes the rest. "That's nice," I thought, never considering that I would actually leave after 20.

Time marches on and 20 years passed in the blink of an eye. The person I was when I started is long gone; a different, more somber, at times cynical person, has taken his place. People who walked in my shoes fought for the 20-year pension deal knowing from experience that 20 years in firefighter time is a long, long time. They knew, as only one who lived the life will ever know, that for some, 20 years is enough. They knew that at 45 or 50, starting a new career is not that easy, or starting a business when everybody else has had a 20-year head start is challenging, to say the least.

I remember sitting in at a critical incident debriefing a few hours after I held two dead infants in my arms. My latex gloves had melted into their skin as their bodies were so hot as I tried unsuccessfully to revive them with my new CPR skills. I bagged the one-year-old—Savannah—while doing compressions on the other, John. It was rough, but it was what I had signed on for.

The guy who brought the babies from the fire to me was a 20-year veteran firefighter, a tough guy by all accounts. When it was his turn to speak he filled with tears and couldn't. He hung his head and valiantly tried to express his feelings, but couldn't. He left the room. A few months later he was gone. Retired. He told me much later that it wasn't necessarily that call that did it; it was all the calls leading up to and including that one that finished him. He simply could not do it again.

I should have learned a lesson that day, but mired in the arrogance of youth I hadn't lived enough to sense my own frailty. I was invincible. I thought of him the other day, as I drove home from what I thought was an unremarkable tour. As I neared my street, I thought of the little girl who claimed to have injured her knee and refused to move from the gymnasium floor. Her mother looked on from a distance, annoyed as I tried to figure out what was wrong. No bleeding or deformity, swelling or anything really. She showed me her other knee as a comparison, and I noticed bruises, weeks old on both legs, and both arms, and a haunted look on her face. I let it go. We can't save everybody, and she probably is just an active kid who bruises easily. Or not.

I turned onto my street and had to stop the car. Where was the little girl now? Was she home in her room reading or watching TV, or was she being punished for being a cry baby like the kid a few weeks ago whose mother called us because her son "fell" from his bed—fell and had severe head trauma and curling iron burns on his legs. It took 10 minutes for me to pull myself together before I could walk in my door and not bring 20 years worth of memories with me.

I haven't been sleeping well. It's been going on for months now. Every night that I'm home I'll go into a fitful slumber around midnight, only to be fully awake at 2 a.m. I toss

*and turn for hours, finally getting some relief from my spin-
ning mind at sunrise, only to be back up an hour later. I
grab an hour here and there as time permits, but have no
idea what a full night's sleep feels like, unless it is drug-
induced, but I try to avoid that.*

*What runs through my mind is probably similar to every
other person my age—are the kids really okay, will the bills
get paid, am I truly happy or is this just an illusion, is that
spot on my back the cancer that will kill me or just a mole.
Then I get the ghosts...*

- *The baby run over by the 18-wheeler as it turned the
  corner on North Main and Doyle, dead in the middle
  of the street, the baby carriage twisted and crushed
  100 feet from the body.*
- *The guy buried alive at sunset on Dorothy and his lifeless arm the first thing we dug up.*
- *The 20-year-old guy and his 20-year-old friend dead
  in the front seat of their Mustang at the Atwells
  Avenue off-ramp.*
- *The 55-year old guy who was new at motorcycle riding
  who tapped a rear view mirror, lost control on 195,
  flipped over the Jersey barrier and was crushed by a
  Toyota Camry full of kids. We found his foot later, still
  in his boot.*
- *The 18-year-old tattoo artist found hanging in his
  basement by his roommate.*
- *My friend's brother found hanging in his bedroom closet.*
- *A RISD student found hanging from the wrought
  iron fence at Prospect Park.*
- *The kid found hanging off the side of his house on
  New Year's Eve.*

- *The 55-year-old who told his wife he was going golfing, started his car, didn't open the garage door and died next to his clubs.*
- *The 40-year-old who held up traffic while he considered jumping from the overpass, then did as the crowd that had formed cheered.*
- *The college kid who fell 80 feet to his death the week before Christmas.*
- *The baby who rolled himself into his blanket and suffocated while his dad was napping on the couch.*
- *My friend Kenny who had a heart attack at his third building fire of the day and had to be defibrillated, who came back to life but not the job.*
- *The 17-year-old girl who bled to death in the front seat of a car that had struck a tree while eluding police as her friends picked her pockets of the crack vials they were selling.*
- *The baby born dead and put into a hefty bag.*
- *The woman dead in her kitchen with a bullet hole in her forehead and her three children sitting on a couch in the next room.*
- *The two babies that broke the veteran firefighter.*
- *The eight-year-old deaf girl who broke my heart when I learned she had been prostituting for her foster parents.*
- *The 20-year-old dancer dead in her car after taking all of her pills, and the vomit-covered note on her lap.*
- *The family dead behind the front door as the fire burned out of control behind them.*
- *Delivering a baby in the back of the rescue and having the mother yell get that thing away from me when I handed it to her.*

There are dozens, hundreds more, all waiting for that delicate twilight between sleep and consciousness to come uninvited into my mind. More join the parade every day that I come to work. Just the other week a 23-year-old hit and killed while walking home from a nightclub, a 30-year-old guy shot in the head, back and legs who walked to the rescue and then collapsed.

I am not a machine. I am a simple person who signed on to do a job, and have done it well. If I choose to leave this year, I will do so with my head held high and hope that the pension that didn't matter to me 20 years ago, but has become my lifeline, is still there.

*reprinted with permission from the *Providence Journal*

It wasn't all bad, and I only had fleeting moments of depression, but those moments went deep, and I'd rather they stayed buried.

The gloom dissipated the further from the job I got, and it could disappear completely at times—for example, when one of the dogs ran up to me with a horseshoe crab, a crustacean unchanged since prehistoric times, in his teeth. The dogs weren't haunted by things they had no control over. They simply existed, ran in the sand, and didn't think about the little sea creatures that were plucked from the sand by seagulls, carried to dizzying heights, and dropped on rocks so their innards were exposed and the gulls could feast. They weren't worried about the bodies they had seen, and they weren't haunted by them.

But my dogs were gone, dead before their time. I missed those dogs, more than I could have imagined. Walking on the beach alone just wasn't the same when the most prominent ghosts I saw were a hybrid malamute and a Siberian husky.

Chapter 23

WEIRD GUY WALKING

Cheryl sensed my dissatisfaction with my walks, mostly due to the infrequency of them and the resulting shrinking waistline of my pants. The less I walked, the more my pants shrank. Weird but true. I didn't want to burden her with the real reason I stopped walking to the beach.

"You need to walk more," she mentioned one day when I was moping around the house.

"I have nowhere to go," I replied, quite content to remain moping.

"Walk to the gym, you used to love to do that."

"I don't have time."

"Make time, you have to stay healthy."

"I am healthy."

She glanced at my expanding belly, then into my eyes. I betrayed nothing, knowing that any sign of weakness would lead to more salad and less meat.

"We should get a dog, then you would walk more."

"And, maybe people wouldn't hide their wives and daughters when the tall, weird guy who walks alone came by their house."

"That's your imagination."

"It most certainly is not. A middle-aged man walking alone through a neighborhood makes people worry."

"No it doesn't, what is the matter with you?"

"I know how people think."

"People, thankfully, do not think the way you do."

"Then how come nobody says hi when I'm walking by myself, but when I had the dogs with me, everybody did? People in cars would actually stop and ask what kind of dogs they were."

"Because people like dogs more than they like people."

She had a point. And she knew that she was going to get me a dog. And that dog would be Mr. Wilson.

I think if we had been able to stay in the house we loved, walking wouldn't have been an issue. I had a giant yard to walk around in; gardens; a cabana with all the amenities, which I dubbed "the Love Shack," next to the pool; a big shed full of shovels and rakes and dirt in bags and fertilizer and hoses and parts of things that I had no idea what they were; a giant dog pen; horseshoes; a badminton net; and plenty of weeds to pull. Plus, I was a familiar face in the neighborhood, and people would remember me as the guy who used to walk the dogs, not the weird guy walking.

That house was magical, and we missed it. Moving can be fun and adventurous when you are doing so for the right reasons. Getting a bigger house, a better neighborhood for the kids, a different location for a new job—those are all great reasons to move. Not so great is moving because you fear the stairs you once flew up and down, carrying basketfuls of laundry. Stairs shouldn't be a big deal to people in their thirties and forties, but they were, and they had to go. Along with the stairs went the accumulation of years of living, collections of things, and the result of countless hours decorating—something we had loved to do together.

Our old house had been Cheryl's house, and her touch made it more than a cape with a nice yard. It had soul. At Christmastime, I would come home from work, exhausted, and find the tree up, the banisters wrapped with garland, lights everywhere, and best of all, seven Christmas trees. Every room had its own tree. Some were big, some were small, some bore fruit, others birds, and the big one held the family treasures.

Often, I would get home before sunrise, when everybody was in bed, and I would walk around the place I called my home, looking at the things on the walls, the perfectly decorated windows, the flowers and plants just right. I would see my dogs in the yard, know my family was there, too. Knowing that they were in such a good place made being away from home four days a week a little easier. Overtime was great for paying the bills, but the time spent away from home was a poor trade-off.

If I could do it over, I would work less, so when I walked through my house when everybody was asleep, I would feel more a part of what I loved so much.

Chapter 24

WOLVES

Zimba was a wolf. Literally. His mom was a Canadian timber wolf and his dad an Alaskan malamute. The person who bred the two was involved in sled dog racing and toured New England with her team. One day, an idea formed in her head—"what if I were to breed a wolf with a dog, thus creating a super sled dog?"

So she did. One of her colleagues from "up north" owned a female timber wolf, if owning a wild animal is possible, and sold it to her. She already had a male malamute, so she introduced the two and let nature take over. They had a litter of pups to go along with the rest of her sled dogs. When they grew up, she harnessed them with the others and began training. The dogs freaked out when they smelled the wolves, the wolves wanted no part of the harness, the training ended nearly as soon as it began, and the hybrid sled dog team was disbanded before its first race. The year-old wolf-hybrids were given away, and more likely than not ended up in a shelter somewhere, because wolf-dogs are terrible pets and even worse sled dog team members.

For some inexplicable reason, she tried again. This time she was in possession of a litter of four. Within weeks, the wolf-dogs had learned to howl. A few weeks later, they howled so loud that the neighbors heard them and complained to the authorities. The first time around, they had given her a pass, but not this time. Our hometown is a residential area; most homes sit on quarter-acre lots. There's not a lot of howling room in suburbia and a wolf pack stands out.

Our daughter, Danielle, just a pup herself at the time, learned through the neighborhood grapevine that a raid was imminent and a group of wolf-dogs was in jeopardy of being terminated, as the law prohibits wild animals inside city boundaries. Being a kindhearted soul, she took it upon herself to liberate one of the pups and save him from his fate. She brought him home and introduced us to our new pet.

It was not love at first sight. His ears were too big, his nose too pointy, and his teeth too long. He was a gangly thing, clumsy, silly, and weird. I had wanted a dog for a while, maybe a hound dog, one of those sleepy critters that sits next to you on the porch when you sip lemonade on a hot summer's day or sleeps next to the fire in winter. What I want and what I get are often two entirely different things, but what I get is sometimes exactly what I need, and what I want is maybe not such a great idea.

Cheryl and I agreed to let Danielle keep him but only until a suitable home could be found. Zimba decided our home suited him just fine and went to work capturing the affection of every member of our family. Within a week, he was one of us. Zimba escaped prosecution and termination and was granted permanent refuge status for as long as he remained a member of the Morse household. Danielle was not as fortunate. She had to take care of him.

True to his nature, Zimba turned out to be more than we could handle. It took us a year to figure it out, with a few ruined couches, a number of car interiors, numerous broken windows and screens resulting from Zimba's insistence on getting in, not out. We put him in the yard; he jumped through a window to get in. We put him back out; he found a different way to breach our security, barreling through a screen door or charming Brittany or Danielle. He was quite the charmer, with big brown eyes, nice eyelashes, a natural, toothy smile that melted the hearts of women everywhere . . . once they got past the fangs.

He wasn't a bad dog. He was a good wolf. Wolves do not belong in captivity, even half-wolves. It was heartbreaking, but after living with him for nearly a year, Cheryl and I decided he had to go. Danielle reluctantly agreed. He was a gentle beast, and I never worried about him attacking anybody. He lived with us, slept in Danielle's bed, and bonded with us the way only a pack animal can. But he was a handful, and a big handful at that. We had to come up with a way to find him a place. But how, and where? It would be difficult finding him a good home. Like many animals, hybrids can be unpredictable and dangerous in the wrong hands, and there is no rabies vaccine approved for them. The animal shelters in Rhode Island would be required by law to euthanize him, so that was out of the question. We were truly stuck, and we tried to make the best of living with a half-wild animal while searching for an appropriate place for him.

"I found the perfect place for Zimba," said Cheryl one fine day. Our wolf-dog had been particularly busy lately, doing things that wild animals in captivity do. The weather was perfect for fixing screens, windows, and door frames.

"Me, too. I dug a six-foot hole in the far corner of the yard."

"The Loki Clan Wolf Refuge," she said, ignoring me. "It's in New Hampshire, and they let the animals run free in acre-sized pens. They live like they were supposed to, in packs with other wolves."

"Real wolves will eat him for dinner," I said, as Zimba rested next to me, his eyelids fluttering as he went off to dreamland.

"It says that each refugee is placed into a pack with wolves or wolf-dogs with similar temperaments."

I thought about our predicament: I didn't want to let Zimba go, but knew that something had to be done.

"Let's try it."

I had grown ridiculously fond of him, as had everybody who knew him. He was a gentle giant, mischievous, daring, exotic, and fun. We would miss him.

It took a few weeks to make the arrangements, and when the crying was mostly over, the day was set. We decided to take two cars: Zimba would travel with Danielle and her friend Dave in one car and Cheryl, Brittany, Stephanie, one of Brittany's friends, and I would drive in my Jeep Cherokee. We had bought a Dogloo for Zimba, thinking he would love nothing more than to make it his home. He didn't and it was never used. We strapped it on top of the Jeep, hoping that somebody at the wolf refuge would use it.

Thus, "I am not the Alpha Dog Transport" was formed. It was a short-lived transport company, and the trip was a load of fun. The kids created a new game during the journey. Whenever we made a stop, one or more of them would reach into the empty igloo strapped to the luggage rack on the roof of my Jeep and comfort the imaginary dog inside. People would stop in their tracks, look shocked, and shake their heads, wondering how we could be so careless, transporting our dog that way, but nobody said a word. My crew continued that little charade as we drove up Route 95 toward New Hampshire, leaning out of the windows and calling to the dog in the igloo until they grew bored with that game and started playing license plate games.

We invented "Match the driver"—others may also play the game, but we started it, you know—and it has passed many a long highway hour. Rhode Island license plates typically have two letters followed by three numbers, US 327 for example. I would begin the game with a brilliant, "Underwear Smeller," and Cheryl might offer something equally intelligent, such as "Underarm Sweater," and the kids would take it from there. Swearing was permitted, but only if it was funny enough to make somebody laugh, and gratuitous profanity was strictly prohibited. Other states had more letters on their license plates, and the more letters they had, the better the descriptions of the drivers. It was goofy, but it made the trip a little more enjoyable.

It took nearly four hours of hard highway travel—Rhode Island is a small state and its inhabitants are not seasoned travelers—but the exhausted crew and confused wolf-dog finished their journey with only ten or twelve bathroom-food-coffee breaks and twice that many disgusted looks from people who were tricked into believing the family dog was traveling on the roof. Traveling is not for the weak. Our journey was long and filled with danger, but we persevered and entered the Loki Clan Wolf Refuge at three o'clock on a Saturday afternoon, ready to leave Zimba with the wolves.

Chapter 25

LOKI

The Loki Clan Wolf Refuge is located in the Mount Washington Region on the Maine–New Hampshire border. Fred Keating founded the place, and his mission is to provide a place for wolves and wolf-hybrids to live out the remainder of their days as closely as possible to the way nature intended. One of Fred's favorite quotes says more about the situation faced by wolves and wolf-hybrids in a few words than volumes of books ever could:

"If you cannot give me a place to live, at least give me a place to die." —Chief Joseph

We were a different kind of wolf-dog owner. We rescued one from certain death, tried to live with him, found we could not, and tried to find him a place to live and die. People should not own or breed wolves with dogs. It's not fair to the creation that comes from such a union.

Fred's mission is to create one-acre pens in which to introduce wolf-dogs and let them form their own packs, and establish their own order within the pack. These dogs all came from people who had no use for them and who had abandoned them. A wolf pack is a strong family unit, with an alpha male and an alpha female in charge. The rest of the wolves are members of the pack. If they are not accepted by the pack for whatever reason, the rest of the wolves ostracize the one that doesn't fit until he slinks off and becomes a lone wolf or finds a different pack to be part of. It's a tough world, but it works, and wolves have survived in some of the world's harshest environments for thousands of years.

Zimba was the alpha male in our house, or at least he thought he was. I thought I was, too, but it was really Cheryl. It made for a difficult hierarchy. When we arrived at the Wolf Refuge, it was clear that neither Zimba, me, nor even Cheryl was the alpha anything. Fred was the head honcho, and that was that. We city folk, as he liked to call us, had brought poor Zimba to the hairdressers before his journey—Cheryl and Danielle's idea, not mine—and he sure did look pretty when we arrived. No wolves were in sight, and nobody howled, but I could sense wildness in the air. Fred and his partner, Amy, lived in a mobile home on the outskirts of his land and had all the necessities and a little more. It was comfortable.

We tied Zimba to a tree outside and went in, all six of us, and told Fred our story. He didn't say much, listened well, and made his decision quickly. He agreed to take Zimba and thought he knew the perfect pack to introduce him to. We went outside, and Fred approached Zimba, who rolled onto his back in the submissive pose, just like the books said he would, though this was never even something he considered doing at home. Fred looked at his teeth, felt the top of his head, and shook his own head when he smelled the lovely perfumed soap the groomer had used, but ultimately gave Zimba the permission to stand, not by saying so, but by using some ancient secret body language that only Fred and Zimba understood.

"He's a wolf alright," said Fred. "About 40 percent."

"I think he's at least half," I said, offended that my wolf-dog was more dog than wolf.

Fred ignored me.

"See the black gums, that's wolf markings, and the point on his head too. No mistaking those eyes, but his coat leads me to believe that he's a girlie wolf." He smiled, and we knew then things would be okay.

Amy showed us some photographs of the animals living at the refuge. She took photography seriously, and had her images made into professional quality prints. Her skill with the camera created magnificent representations of the tenants. They looked like wild animals in the photographs. No sign of the fencing that kept them contained was visible. Zimba did not look anything like a wild animal. City living takes the rugged right out of a man (or dog), I suppose. We agreed to leave Zimba at the refuge overnight with Fred and Amy. The plan was to leave him chained outside the fence of the pack that Fred thought he would best fit in with, let them sniff and snarl and whatever wolves do, then we would come back in the morning. We had made arrangements to stay at a local motel in nearby Freyberg, Maine. It took us a while, nobody wanted to leave, and the longer we stayed, the harder it became.

The only thing Fred asked for from us was a little help erecting fences. Danielle's friend Dave and I agreed to spend the next day at the refuge, working. Fred gave us the once-over with his eyes, the wrinkles on his face growing even deeper when he assessed his crew; the laugh lines deep, frown lines not so much.

"You'll do," he said, doubtfully. After the horrible goodbye period with Zimba—which Fred and Amy had to break up, or we would have slept next to him outside of the pen—we drove away.

Zimba cried and howled like I had never heard him, even worse than when the fire trucks went by the house. When the wolves that lived in the mountains heard his mournful howling, the crisp air came alive with the magical song of the wolf packs that until then had remained silent. A chorus of wolves escorted us off the property, and Zimba's voice was silenced by the overwhelming symphony that surrounded us. It was a difficult drive down the dirt road that led us back to civilization. The night wasn't much better.

Chapter 26

BUILDING FENCES

Morning came, and we returned to the refuge as soon as we could. Zimba was right where we left him. It looked like he had a long night as well, and I nearly untied him, put him in the Jeep, and drove away. His expressive eyes begged us to load him up, put him in the igloo on the roof if necessary, and get him the heck out of there. We had decided that Dave and I would stay for the day and help Fred erect the fencing while Cheryl and the girls went to nearby Conway, New Hampshire, to do some shopping. All their thoughts would be with Zimba, though, and I doubted they would enjoy their shopping trip. We all toured as much of the refuge as we could and the wolves came close. Fred opened a gate and let us get close enough to touch a few of the tamer ones. It was an amazing experience, but there was work to be done, so Cheryl and the girls reluctantly left the refuge and headed into town. I'd say Dave and I got the better part of the deal; the mountain air was fresh and we were surrounded by wolves.

Morning had barely broken when we got to work. Fred brought us into the heart of the refuge where we saw some of the other packs of wolves up close for the first time. They were shy, most of them stayed out of sight, but a brave few sauntered to the fence and looked at Fred, waiting for permission before approaching. They certainly were wild—any resemblance to a household pet was long gone. The life they had been living afforded them the luxury of a full coat and their mostly fresh meat diet kept them healthy. Fred and Amy cared for ninety wolves and wolf-hybrids in eight one-acre pens, feeding them, providing fresh water, getting them spayed or neutered and routine veterinarian care. Fred, Dave, and I were going to begin work on a new pen that would house another six to twelve animals.

"We'll try to get a hundred feet done," said Fred, handing out the shovels. Rolls of donated fencing were stacked nearby: eight-foot chain link and posts to fasten it to. Some four-foot fencing accompanied the taller rolls, waiting to be connected to the bottom of the fence once it was raised, connected by clamping little clips to it every few inches, then buried under a foot of earth so that the wolves couldn't dig their way out.

An acre. Eight feet high. Four feet on the ground. Buried. Rocky, rooty land. Dirt so hard we needed pickaxes.

"What are we waiting for?" Dave asked, ready to work. I had seen him work before; his dad owned an excavating company and he is the only person I know who can work as hard and fast as me. And, he's twenty years younger.

So we worked; three men on a mountain, digging, raising, clipping, and sweating. We worked some more, raising posts, raising fences, attaching the two, rounding corners, digging some more, sweating some more. The sun passed over us, cool in the morning, hot by midday, cool again in the afternoon. We ate. It wasn't much, but we drank lots of water. Fred sat on a boulder after a while, but Dave and I kept on digging, lifting, clipping, and raising. By sunset, most of a one-acre pen was finished. All that remained was for somebody to clip the four-foot fencing to the eight-foot fencing and bury it.

Fred was impressed. Zimba was close, my family was returning from Conway, and I was at peace and exhausted. Mountain air and hard work keeps a man rooted in reality, and it feels great.

Chapter 27

LAKOTA

Later, when the girls returned, we had a nice conversation about wolves, wolf-dogs, city boys who could outwork mountain men, and how we could—if we wanted to—take Zimba home. He would need a pen, said Fred, eight feet high, four feet attached to the bottom and buried so he couldn't dig out. He would need a companion animal and would in all likelihood live in his pen and seldom come into the house. We talked it over. The kids were all for it, of course, and Dave agreed to help me with the pen. At first, Cheryl was reticent, but was swayed eventually.

We said goodbye to Fred and Amy a few hours after sunset and returned to our motel room, trying to figure a way to hide a one-hundred-pound wolf-dog.

Zimba needed a companion—a companion that was his who didn't go to work or leave him alone all day. He needed another dog to pal around with, and it didn't take long for us to find the perfect companion.

When we returned from New Hampshire, we took a trip to the Cranston, Rhode Island, municipal animal shelter in our area. It is a well-run place, and the woman in charge loved her animals and did her best to find homes for them, much like every animal shelter I have ever been to.

She wasn't there on the Sunday we visited. Nobody was, nobody but a lonely Siberian husky who was tied to a pole outside the building. We didn't know her name, so we named her Lakota and we took her home. Then on Monday, we brought her back and adopted her properly. Somebody had had enough of her and left her at the pound, no note, no explanation, nothing.

She was a good egg, and Zimba loved having her. And having her. And having her. And she didn't mind, all that much.

For a neutered dog, he sure had a lot of having-hers in him. Eventually, the love lust diminished, and the two lived in a super-fortified pen Dave and I built in my backyard in the middle of a middle-class neighborhood.

We needed an eight-foot high pen, covering as much space as we could manage in our yard, and at the time that meant fifty by twenty feet, six feet high (sorry, Fred, but this isn't a gulag, and I couldn't find eight-foot high chain-link), barbed wire on top, secure fencing buried underground and attached to the upright fence, a heavily secured gate with a sixteen-inch layer of concrete at the base, video surveillance monitored twenty-four hours a day, motion-activated lighting, and audible devices should the animals breach the inner security system. The pen itself was surrounded by five feet of stockade fencing, with an electric wire running along the top. I had to remove the razor wire because I nearly bled to death every time I forgot it was there. The electric fence hurt plenty when I accidentally bumped into it but at least it didn't leave scars. Cheryl caught me digging a moat around our property and made me stop, or we would have had our own little island in the middle of a middle-class neighborhood.

The dogs frolicked by the sixteen- by thirty-two-foot pool by day, went for walks in the evenings with their dad, and ate expensive dog food, beef bones, and whatever they could lure into their lair by night. I still cannot believe that squirrels, skunks, opossums, and raccoons would venture into their kingdom. Most escaped with a few cuts and bruises, but some ended up as snacks for my fuzzy little friends. After her inauspicious beginning—most dogs are not left tied to a post in front of the dog pound—we learned to love Lakota for who she was, and not simply for being Zimba's companion. She had a kind, gentle heart, lots of fur, and one eye that was half white and half blue. She loved attention, if it was from us all the better. Zimba wouldn't let her out of his sight, but that grew old eventually, and she craved human companionship.

We gave her what we could, and the dogs had a good life—not quite what was considered normal, but better than euthanasia. For the first few years, they lived with us, and somehow managed to sleep on our bed and be part of the daily activity of the house. They left a lot of fur, but Cheryl could vacuum every day then, so it wasn't a big problem. When it became a problem, they had to stay outside. I was at work nearly all of my waking hours, the kids were in and out, and as time passed, Cheryl couldn't do all the work she once did. It happened slowly, but eventually they spent more time outside than in, especially at night and when we had company.

They had the run of the yard all day, though. Their favorite thing to do was chase each other around the pool, through the gardens, over the horseshoe court, around the pen, and then rest by the water's edge, panting until one of their servants brought them a bowl of water and a beef bone.

We bought the marrow bones from a local butcher; they were big cow leg bones, I think, and came in eight- to twelve-inch sections. Cheryl would cook them in a big pot of boiling water, but only after I cut them to size, sometimes in half, sometimes in thirds.

"Did you cut the dog's bones yet?"

"Aren't there any in the freezer?"

"You know there aren't. Why do you wait until the last minute?"

"Have you ever cut marrow bones?"

"How hard can it be?"

"The bones are slimy and gross, and I have to secure them on the vise downstairs. Then when they are in tight, I have to cut them with a wood saw. It takes forever and blood and marrow gets all over the place."

"You don't cut yourself every time."

"Not my blood, the bones' blood!"

But they had their bones, every day. It was our way of making up for them having to live in the yard, Lakota especially. She was sweet and would have been a good house pet, but circumstances led her previous family to abandon her, and her mischievous ways would have more likely than not ended her right back at the pound if a different family had adopted her, so we liked to think that she was right where she belonged.

Zimba liked her more than she liked Zimba, and for a seventy-pound husky, she held her own against a one-hundred pound wolf-dog. It is amazing to see how the animal kingdom mirrors humanity, relationship wise. Lakota was the ruler of the roost, until Zimba felt like overthrowing the queen and a fight would ensue, followed by a few days of separation, then reconciliation. We knew things were back to normal in the pen when the dogs chased each other around the yard again.

After bringing Mr. Wilson home a few years later, we realized just how good it was to have a dog in our lives again. Rather than taking their place, Mr. Wilson's presence gave us a sense of normalcy and eased the burden we had felt ever since Zimba and Lakota had to leave us forever. "The Dogs" will never be forgotten, but now, with Mr. Wilson's help, they can be remembered fondly.

Chapter 28

SECURITY

It seemed like we were without a dog for a lifetime. A lot had happened in the three years that had passed since we last had dogs to take care of, but Mr. Wilson showed up and then it seemed like he was always there. When we pulled into our driveway that first day, he sensed that he was home and ran under our overhead garage door before it had raised halfway. We had been pre-warned that he was an escape artist and would dig under fences, dart out of door cracks, scale walls, and maybe even trick his captors into letting him go. We did not expect him to escape the world and run *into* the house.

I let him off of his leash and figured the best way to introduce him to the cats was to let him introduce himself. True to form, both cats ignored the invasion, assuming this was a temporary occupation, much like that *other* dog that would spend a few days at the homestead, completely upset their chi, change their dinner hour, and drink their water. Little did they know, Mr. Wilson—unlike Danielle's dog, Kaya, for whom we doggysat occasionally—was here to stay.

He tried befriending the other little creatures for a while. Luna had retreated into the crate and set up her defense of her new cave, and Victoria found her favorite hidey-hole and retreated there. Nothing doing with the cats, he came back to us, and then inspected his new surroundings, and then came back, and then inspected and came back and on and on. He drank the cats' water with gusto, devoured the little bit of food Cheryl prepared for him, and began his reign as king of his castle.

Our yard was secure, as secure as I could make it anyway, and I am an expert at securing yards. When we returned from the Great White North and the Loki Clan Wolf Refuge with Zimba in tow, I learned quickly how to keep a wolf-dog in his unnatural habitat. That was a work of art, and it worked most of the time. Fred had laid down the law pertaining to keeping a wolf-hybrid safe and happy in suburbia, and though we had sold the house with the giant pen years ago, I'd committed Fred's instructions to memory.

Suffice it to say, Mr. Wilson's days of escaping yards were over.

Our yard was secure, as far as I could tell, anyway. The five-foot picket fence would be enough to keep a normal dog in. All I had to do was fill in a few holes around the bottom of the fence, nail a board or two across some broken pickets, and the yard was inescapable.

We sat outside, Mr. Wilson and I, while Cheryl got lunch ready, and I was able to sit on an Adirondack chair in my back-yard—which now seemed like mine for the first time in years—fully content and happy to simply watch my little friend wander around his new home. Whether he realized he was here to stay, I do not know, but I like to believe that at some instinctual level, he knew. He knew he could relax a little and knew that his days of wandering were over.

I closed my eyes and looked toward the sun, feeling the warmth, knowing that winter was over and spring would soon give way to summer, and I had everything I had ever wanted. Living a life beyond my wildest dreams became a reality once I learned to appreciate the small things, and my dreams became grounded in reality. That reality was best experienced honestly and when I took the time to use all five senses—seeing the beauty of a little dog chasing bugs in my yard; hearing the chatter of birds as their yearly mating season reaches its climax; feeling the sun on the skin of my face, arms and hands, warming me emotionally and physically; smelling the faint traces of spring; and tasting . . . well, nothing there yet, but lunch was on the way!

Smack dab in the middle of my happy-to-be-alive moment, an assault on each and every one of my senses appeared. I felt before I saw a twelve-pound weight on my chest. I tasted dirt on my lips as Mr. Wilson frantically licked my face, and I heard myself laughing, really laughing, belly laughing, laughing like I haven't laughed in years, laughing so hard my face muscles hurt.

We had found home, Wilson and me, and it was a good, honest place, a place where laughter came easily. I felt Cheryl watching us from inside the house, and I felt her smile as well. It had been a long time between belly laughs for both of us, and the little creature who Cheryl had introduced into our lives was already making our lives better.

Chapter 29

MISSED CONNECTIONS

"For a tired little guy, he sure has some spunk," said Cheryl as we watched Mr. Wilson frolic around his new yard, testing the security system, investigating the flower beds for potential digging sites, finding the loosest dirt, moving on to the bird feeders, sniffing around there for a while, and then gracing us with his presence. He finally fell sound asleep under Cheryl's chair.

"We have to be careful with him," said Cheryl. "Did you see how quickly he got comfortable with Brittany? He would take to anybody who showed him attention."

"Yeah, I suppose, he is a friendly little guy."

"I wonder if he would forget us if somebody took him?"

"I wonder if he already forgot Cheri."

He woke from his nap, cocked his head and searched the yard with his eyes, perhaps hoping that miracles came true: Cheri would walk through the gate, and they would play in the yard in Rhode Island like they used to in Arkansas. When he saw that Cheri wasn't coming, he lay his head back down on the cement, closed his eyes and fell asleep, dreaming about whatever it is that dogs dream about.

We sat in the yard for a little while. Mr. Wilson decided he needed some attention, and crawled into my lap and licked my hands while looking at Cheryl.

"Do you think we should get him a friend?" I asked.

"I think we should wait and see, and we can be his friends for now. Things are different; we have more time to spend with him."

She was right, our lives had changed drastically. I had left my job as a firefighter/EMT in Providence, Rhode Island, five years earlier than I had planned, but what good is planning, anyway, when life keeps coming at you? John Lennon once said life is what happens when you're busy making plans . . . or something like that. And if that ain't the truth, nothing is.

My job—which I'd held for twenty-two years—cost us a lot. It nearly cost us us. Eighty-hour weeks, most of the time not at the station but responding to 911 calls from the citizens of Providence, took its toll on me. I lost my perspective and forgot that the people who needed me the most were right under my own roof and in my yard. Those were the people who just needed me to be me, and part of them, and weren't looking for anything else—no help, no handouts, nothing but companionship and somebody to share this life with.

A sense of loss descended upon me while thinking of all the time I spent away from home. Even when I was home, I wasn't really there. The ghosts of Zimba and Lakota, lost, running around the yard that we now occupied, chasing rabbits, sleeping under the stars, their doghouses the only shelter they had, wondering if this was going to be their home, and . . . would it last? They had missed their real home—the one with the giant pen, and the pool, and the fences that kept them in but also kept the world out—and so did we.

Life comes fast, and all the time we spend making plans is time wasted when those plans don't take into consideration the very real fact that the future is unpredictable. When you least expect, it everything changes, and your legs are taken from under you, you're working a million hours trying to compensate for the loss, and the connection between husband and wife is damaged. That damage seems irreparable, and the dogs you love are lost in the ensuing shuffle. They live their lives estranged from their family, uprooted from the life they knew and loved and, after three tries, find themselves in a little yard without a pen and a mom and dad who don't talk anymore, who have forgotten them.

But somehow, the bones kept coming. It was the least we could do.

Chapter 30

MOVING

Cheryl watched from inside the house as Mr. Wilson ran around the yard, and I sat contentedly in my lawn chair. Adopting Wilson had been a risk—a big one. She knew her disease was progressing and her mobility would decrease as the months and years moved on. Caring for a dog is not an easy task and not something to be taken lightly. Zimba had been a chore, and when we made the decision to bring him back from the Loki Clan Wolf Refuge, her multiple sclerosis was manageable. There are three levels of disability from the disease. The first is relapsing remitting, where the person with the disease experiences flare-ups of symptoms that could last a day or two or even a week or more. Things like fatigue, optic pain, weakness, and in some cases near paralysis attack the person, then relent, leaving them confused and bewildered, but resuming some semblance of normalcy. Most people begin their MS trip with relapsing remitting, then move on to secondary progressive, where the disease is on the attack, and the flare-ups never let up, and the person senses a diminishing level of alertness, partial or total weakness, and difficulties with just about every aspect of leading a normal life. Some people stay in the secondary progressive form for good, others take the disease to the next level, primary progressive. A diagnosis of primary progressive MS is a tough one, as the life the patient once knew is most surely over.

Cheryl knew her disease was moving from relapsing remitting when we saved Zimba, but had faith things would be okay and that I would not let her down.

After hanging on for many years, her symptoms worsened, and she knew we had to leave what had become a beautiful home, our home, and a great place for the dogs and kids. It was horrible, leaving that place, but we did. We moved a world away from our friends and neighbors, even though it was only a few miles, and took the dogs with us. We built another pen, only this one not as nice, not as fortified, and not nearly as much fun. Cheryl blamed herself, I blamed Cheryl, and a long period of discontent followed. I pretended to understand, but she was very good at hiding her symptoms, so I never knew how much of her the disease had taken. The house we bought was a disaster; I hated it but insisted we stay and make it work. Cheryl hated it and knew it would never work. The dogs hated it but kept that information to themselves. Everybody was miserable.

We had always wanted to live in a bungalow—until we lived in a bungalow. The garage was fifty feet away from the house, and there were six steps before entering the one-level living space. The kitchen was enormous, and that's great when you can walk, but take the legs away and the spacious kitchen becomes a barren desert and cooking a fancy meal becomes a mirage. The bedrooms were too small, the dining room too big, the bathrooms outdated, and the basement was haunted. Having never lived in a haunted house, it took me a while to realize I was living in one, but the dead people in the basement knew and took every opportunity to give me the creeps. Brittany knew, I knew. Cheryl thought we were nuts, but the dogs seldom entered the house in the two years we lived there, not because they didn't want to come in, but because they knew, too.

We moved out of there after renovating nearly every inch of the place, installing a new heating system and new garage doors, updating the electrical, remodeling the kitchen, plastering and painting walls, and refinishing the floors. I think we did the ceilings, too, and the deck. We lost a ton of money in the process and rented a nice little place after the people who bought our home took over and we couldn't find the right house to buy. We made the mistake of buying the wrong house once; it was a giant mistake and caused a lot of hurt and misunderstanding, which led to anger, resentment, and isolation.

Renting a place was necessary, and we stayed in our best friend's parents' home for six months. It was Tara's house, the place where she had grown up, where her parents had lived for years. Her father passed away at fifty, then ten years later her mom followed. The house was empty, and needed somebody to look after it, so we took it. It was a good time. We did a little healing—not complete, but a beginning—and the dogs had a nice area next to a shed to live in, they had their dog houses, and they had people to bring them bones. Every day that I could, I walked them to the beach.

We finally found a nice place that had to be done over again, but the garage was attached, and we turned a breezeway into a family room and the second of the two-car garage into a laundry area with a half-bathroom. We did the floors and walls and ceilings over and tried to make it home. It was a few streets over from the place we had been renting, so the beach stayed close.

The moves took a lot more than all of our money; they killed our spirit as well. Trying to start over in the middle of life with a debilitating disease and depression brought on from workaholism is not easy but we managed. We eventually settled where Cheryl now stood, watching the husband she was starting to love again play with the dog she had adopted.

"This might actually work," she said, and joined us.

Chapter 31

MORNIN', DUTCH

It was nice having a dog underfoot, and we played with him for the rest of the day, fed him again, and then settled down for the night. Mr. Wilson would sleep next to our bed in the second bed that we bought him, the first now firmly entrenched in Luna's lair and out of reach. Or so we thought.

We had made the decision to keep him off of the people bed prior to the arrival of the little cotton ball, who then put his paws on the edge of the bed and peered at us while we watched TV. Eventually, we relented and let him up with the big people, and he snuggled right in. The wood shavings that lined the crate he occupied during his journey from Arkansas were gone, but the aroma lingered, reminding me of the hamster cages we had filled with a series of little fuzzy things when the kids were little. Hamsters are funny; I still remember Happy, my first pet, and George, our kids' first. Mr. Wilson's smell was comforting, and he snuggled between us, his warmth extending to us both and his very presence simply great.

In the morning, we let him outside to do his business, and he quickly busied himself with that and investigating his new yard again. I saw that my friend from across the street was sitting in front of his garage on a lawn chair. He looked good, all things considered, and relaxed. His was a presence on my street since we moved here, always outside, always eager to help with whatever I was doing. He was injured as a result of his employment in the construction trades and was always home. We had some good times during the all-too-frequent blizzards that have plagued New England these last few winters, using our snow throwers to clear some of our elderly neighbors' driveways. Men are at their best when there is a job to do, and physical activity takes the empty space that no longer needs to be filled with conversation. We just don't have that much to talk about, and exertion is much easier than the mental effort that conversation takes. I walked across the street, up the driveway, and sat next to my neighbor.

"Mornin', Dutch."

"Hey, nice day."

"Yeah it is."

We sat in silence for a minute, and I couldn't help but remember my father, who had died from cancer some twenty years earlier. His voice had been similar to my fifty-seven-year-old neighbor's— it was unmistakable, higher pitched than usual and filled with fear. Fear of the unknown, fear of the known, and fear of dying. It was a dead man's voice, and the man speaking in that tone knew time was short and would end long before he was ready.

"How are you feeling?"

"Like I'm dying."

That's because you are, I thought, but kept it to myself, not that it mattered in the big scheme of things.

He told me so himself, a few weeks earlier. I hadn't seen him since the last big storm in December and had missed him, not so much as a friend, but more as a presence in my everyday life. We were friends of location: the proximity to each other and the similarity of age and experience a common bond, but other than that, we had little in common. But it was a good relationship, and it was comfortable. I knew we would never be best friends, and so did he, and we were good with that.

In March, I had watched through my kitchen window as he lumbered across his yard. One of our neighbors is a retired doctor, and I watched Dutch slowly but persistently make his way to the doctor's house.

"Dutch doesn't look so good," I said to Cheryl as I washed the grinds from my coffeemaker down the sink.

"Where has he been?"

"Inside, I guess. Looks like dead man walking now."

"Maybe the winter has him depressed."

"Yeah, maybe."

But I knew. I knew it as much as I know the sun will rise in the morning and set in the evening. I knew he was sick, really sick, and knew that he knew it, too. I could tell by the way he walked across his yard, toward the doctor's house. Had I not known him prior to that walk, and hadn't known the vivacious man who helped anybody who asked—and many who didn't—I wouldn't have known what I did. I hoped I was wrong, but knew I wasn't. I have seen too many people take similar walks, and the look is unmistakable. Cancer. He had it in his kidney, his lungs, his bones, and in his head.

We sat in comfortable silence for a little while, just enjoying the warmth from the sun that had been in hiding all winter. For him, there wouldn't be many more moments like this, and I wondered how to make myself appreciate each and every moment as if mine were numbered as well. I suppose it's impossible to do, until it's true.

From across the street came a white blur, all legs and floppy ears running toward us at breakneck speed, as if the devil himself were chasing him. He ran toward us, his crooked smile filling his little face, and jumped onto my lap. He wiggled around and licked and panted, all proud of himself for escaping solitary confinement and joining the party.

"Who's that?" asked Dutch, his voice sounding a little more normal.

"This is Mr. Wilson, and he's a very bad boy!"

"Mr. Wilson, huh, he's a smart one," said Dutch, and then he extended his arms—arms that a few months ago could throw a two-hundred-pound snow thrower into the back of his pickup and now could barely hold their own weight—and Mr. Wilson wiggled away from me and launched himself into his arms. He licked his face and squirmed around until he was comfortable. When he was relaxed, he rested, and then Dutch relaxed, smiled, closed his eyes, and drifted off to sleep, a puppy on his lap, a friend of convenience nearby, and the sun warming his face.

He looked at peace, and even though I had only been awake for an hour, I dozed with him and Mr. Wilson. The moment only lasted a little while, but it was a great moment, and if not for Mr. Wilson, would not have been nearly as great. Sometimes it takes a third party, one that has no baggage, opinions, false promises of hope, or silly things to say to break down the barriers we build and let the simplicity of breathing and enjoying each other's company set in.

I didn't even stop to think how he got out of the yard; I was too happy to have him with us.

Chapter 32

SECURITY BREACH

When our visit with Dutch was over, we returned to the yard and I began the investigation into the security breach. Mr. Wilson plead the fifth and wouldn't budge, even through extensive bribery. He was a clever one, that little escape artist, and had perfected the "who, me?" look. I led him around the perimeter of the grounds, searching for clues, keeping a close eye on my prisoner, looking for a guilty glance when and if we came close to his escape route, but he wasn't giving up his secret anytime soon. After three passes around the yard, I gave up and sat in my chair—our chair, that is—and Mr. Wilson joined me, standing on my stomach and chest as I relaxed.

"Where have you guys been?" asked Cheryl, poking her head out the french doors that opened from our dining room into the backyard.

"We were visiting Dutch," I said, keeping the escape secret for now. No sense worrying the wife when there was little she could do to rectify the situation.

"How is he feeling?"

"He's sick, I doubt if he'll see the summer."

"That bad?"

"Yeah, he's in tough shape. I can't believe how fast, seems like just yesterday we were throwing snow."

"I feel bad for Nick."

"Yeah, me, too."

Nicholas was Dutch's twelve-year-old son. He was a quiet kid, shy around us but always polite. He shot baskets at the bottom of our driveway, using one of those backboard-and-net contraptions that appeared one day last year.

"You coming in?"

"Yup, in a minute."

We had developed a routine that we tried to follow strictly, but some days our routine fell apart. It was difficult; we had spent the last year accumulating physical therapy equipment and medical devices and had spent at least two hours every day trying to repair the neurological damage that Cheryl's MS had caused. There was plenty of damage to repair, and we had been working on repairing it for a few years, with some success. If the body can damage itself with disease, we see no reason for it not to be able to repair itself. It just makes sense, when you think of it logically.

Every cell in the human body replaces itself every seven years, so we're going to replace the bad ones with good, healthy ones, and the best way to do that is to feed the body what it needs most to thrive: vitamin-rich and antioxidant-laden food that is absolutely boring, bland, and without an iota of soul. Kale is our mainstay and has been for a long, long time. We have had plain kale, baked kale, kale chips, sautéed kale, kale on a stick—all kinds of kale. I even grow it in what I love to call Honest Mike's Organic Garden. It's not really organic—the soil hasn't had five years to just sit without fertilizer and insect killer, and I use fertilizer and grub control on my lawn, which is right next to the garden—but it's the closest thing to the real deal that I can pull off. Honest. We cut up the kale, put it in our smoothies, and drink 'em every day. Even if we don't cure MS, we will probably live forever.

In addition to our diet, we also do something called neuromuscular electrical stimulation. Every morning, we connect sixteen electrodes to areas of Cheryl's body where the nerve damage has made it difficult to move without outside stimuli, and then turn on a neuroelectrical stimulation unit. The current flows through the wires and into the electrodes, into the muscle fibers, creating an involuntary stimulus that keeps the body moving. Just to prove I'm an idiot, I have on more than one occasion hooked the unit up to myself and turned the power on all the way, just to see how it felt. It feels like one would expect it to feel—like you just stuck a butter knife into the toaster while you were standing in a tub of water.

But all of that could wait two seconds; I still had to figure out how a tiny little dog had managed to escape my elaborate defense system on the first day of confinement. It took the big dogs a couple of days to get out of their secure enclosures, and I was new at the game then.

The answer was so simple, it eluded me. The key words were *tiny little dog.* I was good at keeping big dogs in, not little ones. I refocused my search of the perimeter and there it was, big as day, one of the pickets from the stockade fence was missing the piece at the bottom. A space no bigger than three by six inches existed, and judging from the scratches in the dirt and on the wood, old

Mr. Wilson had squeezed his way through. He stood a few feet back from the broken fence, watching as I put a rock in front of the opening, never giving a thing away. He looked at me as I secured his escape route. He tilted his head, then ran off to find a bird to kill or something, I'm not sure what.

With that problem solved, I moved on to more pressing issues, with how to cure multiple sclerosis taking the number-one spot on the list. For the next few hours, Cheryl, Mr. Wilson, and I worked on that, and at some level progress was made. Mr. Wilson fit right in to our routine, taking his place on the mat platform table that we had bought for the spare bedroom, sitting next to Cheryl while electric current coursed its way through her body. He watched her, alternating between the window to the backyard where he had made his escape, then to her, keeping her company, and making the whole experience a little more bearable for the three of us.

"He got out of the yard while I was sitting with Dutch," I confessed. Now that I had found out how, Cheryl wouldn't worry about letting him outside.

"How did he do that? I thought you had taken care of the yard?"

"I did, but I forgot that he's little. He snuck through a hole in the fence."

"Did you have to chase him?"

"No, he ran right over to us as soon as he got out."

"He escaped so he could be with you. That's good, I think."

"Yeah, I think you're right."

I hadn't thought of that. He found a way out of the yard not so he could get away, but so he could get closer. He could have run free, frolicking around the neighborhood digging holes and chasing rabbits, but he didn't. He ran as fast as his little legs could carry him right across the street where somebody he had known for less than a day sat with a sick friend. I had no food, no toys, no fun, just human companionship, and he craved it so much that he couldn't think of anything else until he achieved it.

We finished with the electrodes, and he tried to chew the wires, and we didn't mind a bit. It was up to us to teach him the little things; he had already learned the big ones.

Chapter 33

THE GREAT ESCAPE

Danielle called and told us that her friend, Sue—the one who was with us when we picked up Wilson—was having some trouble. Buttons, one of the dogs she had picked up, had escaped. She never made it home from the parking lot off of Route 395. Instead, she slipped out of the car at Sue's mother-in-law's house and ran off before anybody could grasp the leash. All the dogs delivered came with nice, blue slip-proof leashes that had been donated for safety reasons and the dogs could not get out of them. They were simply designed things—just a loop that you put the end of the rope through—kind of like a lasso. I found that Mr. Wilson could easily get out of his; he simply backed up a little and waited for me to look the other way and *voila*! Free dog.

Buttons wasn't quite so clever. She ran away, leash and all. She was clever enough, however, to lull her foster mom into a false sense of security during their ride home from the rest area in Connecticut. Much like Mr. Wilson, she was a perfect little doe during the ride home, convincing the lady in charge that such a sweet little thing would be incapable of any devious behavior.

Fostering a dog is an enormous responsibility, and takes a special person to assume it. I can only imagine how horrible Sue felt when the dog she had agreed to take care of slipped away.

This being her first time fostering for FOHARI, she had no idea what to do after the initial search of the neighborhood came up dry. Buttons had simply vanished. She had to tell the people at FOHARI and didn't know what to expect when she gave them the news.

Much to her delight, there were no accusations or reprimands; rather, they were understanding and offered to help. An adoption event that FOHA sponsored close by had just ended, and ten volunteers came to Sue and Buttons's rescue. They canvassed the neighborhood; calling, looking, calling some more until darkness descended, and then they looked even more. They caught sight of her a few times, but she always managed to slip away. After hours of effort, they stopped the search for the night, but resumed the next morning when even more volunteers joined the search party. They did a good job tracking her and found the entry and exit points where she went into and out of a small wooded area that buttressed the busy plat, but the elusive Buttons remained just out of reach. A dog trap was strategically placed, with bait, but the bait disappeared without a dog in the trap.

The search continued for four days. Finally, the trap worked and Buttons was captured. She still wore the leash that she came with and didn't look at all worse for wear considering her ordeal. Sue left her in the cage and drove her home, where she was introduced to the rest of the family. She mingled nicely with Dingo, with whom she was already acquainted from the long ride in the truck. Dingo wasted no time worrying about Buttons—he had been working on Cassie, Sue's daughter. As days turned to weeks, and weeks into a month, the family changed a little: Dingo was officially adopted by Cassie and was a permanent part of the household. Buttons had relaxed to the point where she no longer tried to escape and was happy living with her foster family.

A woman from Providence adopted her after a while. She lives with her now, and the two get along quite well. Fostering works wonders. Buttons is now a happy pet, a woman has a friend, and Sue's inauspicious beginning had a happy ending.

It didn't take long for Sue to fill the void; two more rescue dogs found their way into her home. Chachi is a ten-year-old Chihuahua with a weight problem who just loves to steal dirty socks, but is also a lot of fun to be with. Then there's Rocket Man, a young fella who loves his little foster family and will make somebody a great pet as soon as they adopt him. There are adoption events all across the country, where fostered dogs are allowed to strut their stuff, and foster families get the chance to have their little friends find a forever home. Chachi gets a little nutty with all the attention, and once gave a little boy a little nibble—no lasting harm was done but he blew his chance of being adopted that day. There are easy adoptions, and not-so-easy adoptions, and Chachi fits into the latter category. There is a person waiting for him, though, and adoption events give the foster dogs the exposure they would never get without them. Seeing a picture on the Internet tells a small part of a dog's story. No expression or mannerisms are articulated, and the character that every dog possesses is not fully expressed.

Even "old and ugly" dogs like Chachi have a place; it's up to us to find it.

Sue's husband thinks she's nuts, but he's a good egg and goes along with all the nuttiness. They don't have a fenced-in yard, and all of the dogs need to be walked, played with, fed, picked up after, and taken to the vet and adoption events, but once the little critters get under your skin, it's tough to get them out.

The volunteers that make FOHARI so special spend countless hours finding homes for homeless pets. There is no brick-and-mortar shelter; every animal under their care is fostered in somebody's home. I had no idea there were so many people willing to help homeless animals until Cheryl found Mr. Wilson. Just having him is enough to make us happy; he fills a void in our lives that we had not acknowledged and were not aware how deep it was until he came into our lives. He didn't make it here by himself, however; he is the culmination of hundreds of hours of work done by people who do so for no reason other than their love for homeless animals. That love transcends the animal itself, and becomes part of the people who are fortunate enough to adopt one of their charges. Love is most definitely contagious, and never dies, and not a bit of love goes to waste. Every ounce of it created and nurtured by these people is now part of the fabric of the universe and every living thing benefits from it.

Our little part of that love was sound asleep, and if dogs could purr, his would be a roar. And if people could purr, the walls might collapse from all the rumbling that was going on inside our home.

Chapter 34

MAGIC

He slept the night through, his warm little body nestled between Cheryl and me, his presence felt, acknowledged, and accepted. Our plan to keep him in his "baby bed," a comfy little doggie mattress if ever there was one, worked for about five seconds. The unspoken language between long-married people confirmed what we both already knew—Mister Wilson would be part of the bed clan: Lunabelle next to Cheryl, Victoria at the foot of the bed, and good ol' Wilson between us. Positions were sure to change as the night progressed, but if all was well, we would sleep through all the maneuvering.

Nobody was allowed under the covers, except of course Mr. and Mrs. Alpha People, and the critters mostly obeyed the rules of the roost—all but Luna, who would slither her way between the bedspread and upper blanket and lay in wait. She liked to think of it as "the tall grass," and would back herself in, poking just her head out, and stalk whatever prey came her way: a foot, a knee, sometimes a hand, whatever moved was fair game.

Now there was some big game for her to hunt, and Mr. Wilson learned right quick to avoid the tall-grass area of the bed. Victoria kept close watch on the festivities and allowed them to go on, as long as she had no part in the hijinks. When it came to nutty behavior, she was the queen, but only when it was completely unexpected and absolutely inappropriate, like a mad dash through the house in the middle of the night, or a hissy fit while being held and petted, or an erstwhile swipe of who- or whatever walked past whatever part of the house she had declared her own.

Our second night with Mr. Wilson was serene; he fell soundly asleep at eleven and didn't stir until seven. We moved him a few times and he didn't blink. At one point, just before lights out, he woke briefly and stood between us, but quickly closed his eyes and fell asleep while standing. He fell to the side, still asleep, and didn't wake until morning.

"I'm taking Mr. Wilson for a walk," I said, once the morning routine was finished, Cheryl's nervous system charged, green smoothies made, and the house relatively picked up.

"Are you going to the beach?"

"I think we are."

"Have fun."

I kissed her goodbye, knowing that she was dying inside, knowing that she would give her left leg just to be able to walk with us, just once more, and see the neighborhood the way it is meant to be seen: walking, breathing the air, listening to the birds, seeing the people come and go—not as an observer, driving a nondescript car through streets that had no meaning, past houses that appeared vacant, but as a walking part of the fiber that makes those streets and houses a living, breathing entity, the place we desperately wanted to call home.

We had left our real home six years ago, and through three moves had yet to make it back. Home is definitely where the heart is, but a broken heart makes a broken home, and mending the heart must come first.

She kissed me back. And it felt good. It felt like things were going to be all right.

Mr. Wilson took to the leash well, and I put the things I had learned into action. I commanded him to sit, and after some downward pressure on his hindquarters, he did. I told him to stay, and he did, as long as I stayed, too. I opened the door that led from our laundry room into our garage and said, "Come," and he was out of the door before the sound of my voice had faded. We repeated the "sit, stay, come" commands, and then I opened the overhead garage door. Those little buttons on the wall work wonders; the door magically lifted as soon as I pressed it. I said the words "Open Sesame," trying to astonish Mr. Wilson with my magical powers. For a dog, everything we do is magical, and he was as impressed with my magical ability to open a door from twenty feet away as he was with my ability to put on a pair of sneakers.

It's a magical world when you're a dog, and you don't question anything—you simply accept that things work, and those two-legged people make them work, and by listening to those people, and ingratiating yourself to them, magical things happen.

I had read that while walking a dog, it is imperative that you lead, keeping the dog close to you, and a little behind. Zimba, Lakota, and I walked as one when the world was ours. It took a long time and a lot of work to get it right, but there was no other way: they had to listen and obey or there could be no walk. Their combined weight was more than mine, and adherence to my rules was imperative, absolute, and the way it was, period.

I tightened the leash, leaving Mr. Wilson no room to wiggle. He walked next to me, happy to be out of the house, curious about his new surroundings and barely able to contain his joy.

"Wilson, heel," I said, over and over as our walk progressed, and he glued himself to the outside of my left leg and kept on walking, some fifty steps to my one, but he had twice as many legs and fifty fewer years on his body, so I figured he could withstand the rigors of a forced march. He did well for a half-mile or so, but began to wander, curiously at exactly the same time I relented and let the leash go from my left hand, giving him six feet to explore along my circumference. He took full advantage of the lapse in training and ran around in circles as we walked forward, sniffing everything, peeing here and there and having a ball. Dogs get depressed, I'm sure of it, especially when nobody pays them any attention, but they are capable of irrepressible joy as well, and it's easy for them—all they need is somebody to lead the way.

As determined as I was to teach "heel" to Mr. Wilson, I found it increasingly difficult to do so, not because of him—I was the one who felt silly commanding a twelve-pound bundle of cuteness to bend to my will. It's one thing keeping control of two hundred-plus pounds of dog, quite another to control a little fuzzy thing. I let him explore to the end of his leash. When we made it to Gaspee Point, he decided to glue himself to my leg and didn't wander at all, even as we straddled the water's edge. The whole thing was new to him, him being from Arkansas and all, and having never been to the beach. He walked on seashells while we were there, literally—the shore is covered with shells from all kind of sea creature, like oysters, quahogs, mussels, crabs, and clams. "The River," as my mother used to call it when reminiscing about her days of youth, when her father "worked the river," was closed for fishing and harvesting of any edible shellfish due to pollution, but the bay has been cleaning up for a decade, and the river life has thrived.

Someday, when we get a handle on our waste and they reopen the area to fishing, people will make out like bandits and pull bushels of food out of the sand. Until then, we'll just have to crush the empty shells with our feet and imagine the water and the things that live in it as it was before people inhabited its banks.

We walked the point, about three-quarters of a mile, and returned to civilization, walking up a hill toward the Gaspee Point neighborhood. I managed to keep the ghosts at bay, and the gloom wasn't as oppressive as it once had been. I had a little dog with a giant heart, and he lightened the load considerably. We had about a mile to go before we got home, and Mr. Wilson was pooped. He was a trooper, though, and stayed by my side as we neared home. About a quarter-mile out, he had enough and laid down in the street and wouldn't get up, so I carried him the rest of the way.

"How was your walk?" asked Cheryl when we returned.

I thought about that for a while and then realized just how my walk was.

"It was great."

Chapter 35

THE LEASH

"The Dogs" and I had walked the same road many times and had walked the beach together. I had let them off the leash when we reached the sand and they ran free. It was the least I could do, and they enjoyed every second of their time, running into the tic-infested sea grass that rose some twenty feet above sea level and into a bird sanctuary, feet getting muddy, lungs nearly exploding with exertion, and the wild-life scattering before them. It was as close to living in the wild as they would get, and it was enough. They looked over their shoulders often, making sure I was nearby—far enough away, but still close. The leash that tethered us was made of material far sturdier than leather or nylon, and it transcended hundreds of yards.

It was a long walk for a couple of older, fur-covered dogs, and ill-advised in the summertime. We would take shorter walks then, mostly when the sun went down and the heat gave way to the evening chill, circling our block before heading home.

There is something special about letting your dogs off their leashes and knowing that they would wander only so far before zeroing back in. The bond between man and dog is strongest then, when both sides are using their free will and both choose to stick together. Dogs being dogs, they sometimes got loose, and I could yell and hoot and holler and call their names for eternity, but when presented with an opportunity to lose their hearing for a while, they would take full advantage. They never went deaf during a walk when I let them run free though; that only happened when presented with a chance escape from the yard, when somebody left a gate open, or a chance assault on the electric fence after digging through a foot of chain-link.

"Michael! The dogs are loose!" somebody would shout, and the game was afoot.

When they escaped together, it was a straightforward job: Lakota would run forward, no zigs or zags, one direction only, straight ahead. Siberian huskies are born and bred to be sled dogs, and they seldom veer from the path. Alaskan malamute/timber wolves are born and bred to do God-knows-what, but when the Mrs. led the charge, Zimba was sure to follow. When he escaped on his own, which was seldom, him being preoccupied with his other half, he would slink into the mist and ghost walk through the neighborhood. It was truly fascinating to see; he was very good at disappearing into the environment. He even caught a giant salmon during one of his forays into the wilderness. He returned to our yard after an hourlong absence, full of mud and smelling like a dumpster, but between his teeth was the biggest half fish I had ever seen.

Half fish?

The fish was perfectly sliced about twelve inches from the head. The great gray hunter caught a fish alright, caught it right out of the dumpster of the restaurant at the top of our street.

One prison break ended when we received a phone call from a trucking company some four miles from our home.

"Hello?"

"You got two dogs, Zimba and Zimba?"

Lakota had lost her collar and name tags and we had had an extra Zimba, and the rest is history.

"Yes, I do."

"Found 'em on the railroad tracks behind my shop. They're tired but okay."

"Thank you, I'll be right there."

To get to the dogs, I had to circle T. F. Green Airport, which was located a mile from our home. Then I had to cross a bridge, follow an industrial route toward Jefferson Boulevard, drive over another bridge, and then go another mile to where the dogs waited. It was a five-mile trip by car, two and a half as the crow flies—or the dogs run. After they left home base, they ran straight. Lakota in the lead, Zimba following. They ran through a hole in the fence that surrounded the airport, across the landing tarmac and then the runway, which I am quite certain overjoyed the security team, through another hole in the fence on the other side, across Route 1—the busiest state road in Rhode Island—through a small river, up a bank, over the railroad tracks, and into the trucking company's rear lot. Lakota led the charge, of that I am certain.

I brought them home, and they slept all night, I think.

Mr. Wilson seemed to have an adventurous streak in his little body, and I wondered where he might lead me. As much as I loved my dogs, I was learning to like ol' Mr. Wilson, too. I had only known him for a short time, and already he was working his way into the part of my heart I had slammed shut the day Zimba and Lakota were put down.

Chapter 36

SHELTER

There are too many dogs and not enough people who want them. It's a problem—a big one. Living life unaware of the problem or purposefully ignoring it, or seeing it but not processing it, does not mean it doesn't exist. I am guilty of ignoring the problem. My excuse? The problem is too vast for me to solve. There are millions of unwanted pets. I have an extremely addictive personality. When I learn about something, I tend to over-focus on the subject until I ruin my ability to do anything constructive and sap any enjoyment from the activity or learning process.

I worry that the more I know about the fate of the precious lives lived in shelters, the more immersed in that world I will become. Simply learning about something called "happy tail" sent me into a funk that will be with me in part forever. I would rather not think about it, but now that I know what it is, I cannot stop doing so. (Skip to the next paragraph if you're weak of stomach or heart. "Happy tail" occurs when a dog articulates his happiness by his wagging tail—even while confined to a small cinderblock cell—repeatedly against the cement, the tip of the tail becomes raw, and eventually blood seeps out, but the tail still wags, and the walls are covered with sprayed blood.) There is so much that could be done to alleviate the suffering, but how much am I willing to do? How much can anybody be asked to do? The problem is immense, cruel, and heartbreaking. One easy way to fix the problem is to pretend it doesn't exist. Let somebody else worry about it. Think of something else. Do something else. But what if I were to do a little? Volunteer some time, adopt a dog or a cat, maybe foster one or two, write a letter, or go to an adoption event. Maybe then the vision of the bloody wall in an empty cell will recede. Perhaps I can make a difference. Perhaps we all can make a difference, and each of us in our own small way will collectively turn this thing around. I can only hope.

As much as I would like to save all the unwanted animals, I know that it is impossible. What it boils down to is this: people come first. It has to be that way. We simply cannot allow unwanted pets to live their lives on their own. They become feral and a danger to the community. Two types of shelters help: an open admission/kill shelter and a limited admission/no kill shelter. Most municipalities operate open admission/kill shelters, funded with taxpayer dollars. These are necessary evils, though less evil than I originally thought—of course, my original thinking was minimal at best. In my naïve and absurdly optimistic worldview, everything is fair and the well-being of the living creatures entrusted to our care is of utmost importance. In reality, the town- or city-operated "pounds"—short for "impoundment," which means all rights and power now concerning the surrendered or rescued animal belongs to the state—have limited budgets and limited room and are forced to make a lot of unfair decisions regarding the life or death of the surrendered pets. I used to believe that most of the animals that made their way to the pound would be reclaimed by worried owners or adopted into loving homes. I believed wrong.

I have toured the "pounds" many times, sometimes in search of a lost pet, other times looking for a pet to adopt. The pounds in my area are city-run, well-kept, and understaffed by what at first glance appears to be people who are harsh, incapable of loving animals, and borderline monsters. Nothing could be further from the truth.

To accept an animal in their care requires the ability to block out the probability that this is the final destination for the little cutie that made its way into their door. Bonding with that animal is ill-advised for the person taking control of the living, breathing, feeling, and thinking creature that is now under their care. To survive in that environment, walls must be erected and compartments in the heart and mind established; places where the facts are allowed to live separately from the rest of the thoughts and feelings that make us human.

According to the American Humane Society's recent numbers, 56 percent of dogs and 71 percent of cats that enter shelters are euthanized. More cats than dogs are put down simply because fewer cats arrive with owner identification. "Getting rid of" unwanted dogs and cats is something most people don't think about. It is an ugly part of our society—ugly, demoralizing, and heartbreaking. But it must be done; there simply are not enough homes for the dogs and cats to occupy.

The world works in ways in which we have no comprehension. We don't know where all those dogs and cats go because we don't want to know. *I* don't want to know. I want to walk my dogs, listen to my cats purr, pet them now and then, and enjoy their company. I take care of them, bring them to the vet, have them spayed and neutered, and think I have done my part.

And I have.

There are people who do more. They work with the animals, care for them, provide shelter during their last days, and give a little hope that they might be found or adopted. These are not monsters; they are people doing a job so that we don't have to think about the job being done. Perhaps more awareness would prompt people to spay and neuter their pets and not have their cute little doggie or kitty have "just one" litter before doing so. Maybe if people did the small amount of research into shelter animal euthanasia that I did while writing this book, they would smarten up and make sure their pets made no others.

Limited admission/no kill shelters offer temporary places for unwanted pets to stay until they can be adopted. The key words here are *limited admission*. Big, aggressive dogs; sick dogs and cats; and pets that are unadoptable for whatever reason are not welcome here and have only one place left to go: the kill shelter. The end result is that unwanted pets that are unadoptable end up in a kill shelter, and are killed. As much as we want to kid ourselves and be comforted by the existence of no-kill shelters, some things are inevitable, and our best intentions are not good enough. It's enough to make a person crazy, and we have enough crazy people already, so my advice is to do a little to help the situation. Spay and neuter your pets, advocate for the spaying and neutering of everybody's pets, or volunteer whatever time or money is comfortable to a local organization that exists to find homes for unwanted pets and advocates the humane treatment of those who are unadoptable. Sometimes euthanasia is the humane answer; dogs that spend too much time in cells have a tendency to change, they get depressed and hostile, and euthanasia is kinder than an existence with no hope of love or freedom.

There is a place for responsible breeding, I believe, and pure-bred animals are essential to our enjoyment of life and the gift of it. As guardians over existence, humanity owes it to the universe to preserve the individual uniqueness of the animal kingdom. We do not need to let more and more unwanted dogs and cats into the universe, however. We have the ability and power to control to some extent the world around us. We can choose to ignore it, happily go about our business, and let things be, or we can pay a little attention, spay and neuter our pets, and let things be a little better.

Chapter 37

DOG BY GOOGLE

Yesterday's beach walk wore old Mr. Wilson out, so I decided the neighborhood tour would be a better way to acclimate him to his new routine.

"Wilson, come."

Nothing but a nod of his head and back to bed.

"Mr. Wilson, come!"

A little more interest, but not much.

"Come on, buddy, we're going for a walk," I said in my most whimsical voice, one full of promise for a fun-filled day. He ran toward me, jumped up on my legs, and tried to jump into my arms.

"Wilson, down."

More jumping, only higher.

"Mr. Wilson, *down*!" I said, and he sat.

Impressed with my progress, I took our training to the next level.

"Wilson, stay."

And he followed me toward the door.

"Wilson, sit!"

He lay on his back and raised his feet in the air.

"Wilson, come," I said, and opened the door to the outside.

He came.

"Told you he was brilliant," I said to Cheryl, who had joined the training party.

"We need to train him properly."

"I am, didn't you just hear me?"

"I'm serious. He's a great dog. It's up to us to keep him that way. We could easily ruin him."

She was right and I knew it. My tendency to let things go at their own pace and not make waves causes more problems than it solves. Cheryl knew I would be content if the dog came when called and sat every now and then. I never trained Zimba and Lakota thoroughly; they came to me because they wanted to be with me, sat because I spent a day teaching them how to, and ran to my truck when I said "truck," but that was about it. I never made them do tricks, especially not for food, thinking the practice was barbaric. They deserved to eat and not have to perform for their meals.

But this wasn't a half-wild animal; this was a dog who loved to please his masters. He truly enjoyed doing what we wanted him to do. We just had to figure out how to make him understand what we wanted. Teaching a human to think like a dog is as about as easy as a teaching a dog how to think like a human.

"What we've got here is a failure to communicate," I said.

"That's great, Luke," said Cheryl, who was always impressed with my ability to quote obscure things from old movies. "We just have to try and figure it out. I'll Google some stuff while you're gone."

Great. Dog by Google.

"We're in big trouble, Mr. Wilson," I said while clipping his leash to his collar. I used the six-foot nylon one, leaving the twenty-foot extension leash for another day. I wanted to continue teaching him "heel" and needed total control.

"Don't be an idiot, this is important," Cheryl said.

"I know, but Rome wasn't built in a day."

"Famous last words," said Cheryl with a rueful smile as we walked down the driveway and out of sight.

He was a fast learner, I found, and heeled remarkably well when I let him know it was expected. By keeping the end of the leash in my right hand and offering just enough slack for him to be comfortable next to my left leg and a little behind me, we established a comfortable rhythm. He was alert, and cocked his head at every strange sight or sound but stayed the course, happy to be connected to his new master and eager to please. People passed us, some walking dogs, others walking together, talking about whatever it is that couples discuss during their walks around the neighborhood.

I missed Cheryl. Missed her desperately. We once walked three or more miles a day, after spending an hour at Gold's Gym doing bench presses, squats, lunges, one-armed rows, triceps extensions, calf raises, and even more, whatever we could do to stay in shape. I still can't figure out how somebody as healthy as Cheryl could be afflicted with MS; it just doesn't seem fair.

I could talk with Mr. Wilson, though he offered little in return. But his presence was comforting and gave my walk purpose and, sure enough, people who once ignored me when I walked alone now said cheerful hellos and didn't cross the street when I approached. Little kids wanted to pet the dog, and I let them. It's funny how we will pass a stranger with barely a nod, but put them at the end of a dog's leash and they instantly become somebody of interest, somebody approachable, and worthy of a hearty hello and maybe even a little conversation.

I was surprised by how easily I nestled back into my role of proud dog owner. It was as if there had always been a dog with me wherever I walked. Mr. Wilson was completely at ease and enjoyed our walk as much as I did. When we approached home, he perked up and pulled on the leash, eager to get inside now that the walk was done. He had a home, and he knew it, and he hoped it lasted longer than the last one.

Chapter 38

ALL IN A DAY'S WORK

It wasn't long before routines were established, a pecking order determined, and peaceful coexistence returned to our house. Mr. Wilson befriended Victoria, annoyed Lunabelle, charmed Danielle and Brittany, comforted Dutch, and restored a sense of family and hope to our home.

"All in a day's work," he seemed to say, as he went about the business of making everybody he met happy. His presence is impossible to overlook. Few people, and even fewer dogs, make an unforgettable impact on nearly everybody they meet. Mr. Wilson is just one of those people. Or rather, dogs.

On a typical day, he wakes before sunrise, opening his eyes and looking at the people he sleeps with. He sees their still forms in the predawn darkness, hears them breathing, glides into their rhythm, then falls back asleep. He sleeps soundly now; his troubles appear to be behind him. Eventually, that deep sleep becomes a fitful slumber in dreamy twilight time between dawn and sunrise. His bladder is screaming, but the peace in his bed is too wonderful to end. He waits, and one of them stirs, the one with the soft voice. She opens her eyes, feels around the bed until she touches him, and when she does, he can't help himself, he's fully awake. He stands, yawns and stretches, crawls closer, and happily receives the hand that caresses his back and rubs the area over his eyes. He knows that she loves his eyelashes because she tells everybody how great they are, and he bats them at her as she continues to pet him. He has to pee, but that can wait, though not for much longer. Every moment of this bliss is worth the uncomfortable feeling.

A screech and Victoria joins the party on the bed. The big lump stirs, and the sun shines through the blinds and dapples the bedclothes. Then the big cat appears as if by magic, but the magic ends abruptly when she steps on the people and demands to be fed.

We all want to eat, he thinks, *but why can't you just enjoy this moment?* He doesn't know that the cats are secure in their position and have lived with these two people for eight years. They depend on them to be there, and know that they will, so for them this moment is just another morning. He doesn't know what the cats are thinking; he only knows that life at this moment is as good as it will get.

The people stir, the cats jump on and off the bed, the man gets up, throws on a T-shirt and a pair of shorts and says, "Hello, everybody." The cats run for their food bowls—they having the luxury of indoor facilities and are not worried about accidents—and he runs for the door. *Best not pee in the house,* he thinks, *or this party could be over before it has a chance to get started!*

The lady gets up, and the man feeds the cats and lets him out to do his business, which quickly becomes the business of chasing the birds and squirrels that gather around the feeders.

How nice of them to provide me with entertainment, he thinks as he dashes out the french doors, bounds over the herb garden, lands in the middle of some fragrant, dew-covered lavender, and immerses himself in the flurry of flapping feathers as mourning doves, chickadees, tufted titmice, sparrows, and woodpeckers fly away hurriedly. The squirrels, unable to fly, must run—and run they do, up a pine tree that stands nearby, offering coverage from above where hawks circle, and sometimes swoop down and eat the cute little birdies who feed here.

Mr. Wilson knows these things because he is an integral part of the animal kingdom where such things are simply part of the knowledge base that comes with being born an animal. He also knows he can't climb trees, but that doesn't stop him from trying. He barks a little, a nice bark, not high pitched or frantic; rather, a simple *woof*. The animals he is chasing cock their ears and wonder why the dog who chases them barks with a Southern drawl. He barks again, *woof, y'all*, and the animals realize that it doesn't matter how he barks, the meaning is still the same. They will spend however long it takes in the trees until the new intruder is gone, back in the house, and they will only have to watch the skies for predators.

He hears his name, "Mr. Wilson!" and stops his attempt to climb the pine tree and runs full speed toward the man's voice. He runs past their chair, where just a few days ago he sat for the first time and laid on the man's chest, licked his face, and made him laugh; a laugh that was infectious and filled him with joy.

"Breakfast is served!" And so it was, a wonderful assortment of crunchy bits soaked in hot water, topped with some canned chicken.

He stuffs his head into the bowl, gulping it down, licking the bowl as if it were the last bit of food on Earth.

The people are there, watching him, and they are smiling and seem quite happy with him, so he runs toward them, but it's harder to run with his paws sticking to the wood floors. He makes it, though, and jumps on the lady. She picks him up, touches the bottom of his feet, looks at the man, and says, "His feet are full of sap."

But what's a little sticky feet among friends? he thinks as they carry him toward the room where they do their business. He hears running water and before long he is in the tub, his feet are wet, and they are massaging them, all four, and he knows that this is a place he can call home.

Chapter 39

PENS

We sat on the chairs we had bought for the patio—plastic Adirondack replicas, low but comfortable—and watched Mr. Wilson run around the yard. It was quickly becoming our favorite pastime. He took to his new place as if he had always been there. He hadn't, but he liked it just fine.

Zimba and Lakota were not so sure of their new yard when we moved them there. For all they knew, it was just another place they would leave in a year or two. Once they left the big pen with the pool nearby and the happy family in the house inside, they never knew home again.

I had to take their pen down before the people who bought our home moved in, and had arranged to store the posts and rolls of fencing at the house we were buying. Just before closing day, I was allowed access to the property and on a one-hundred-degree day, I erected the dog's new home. It was half the size of the original, no pool, no horseshoe court, no bushes to chase each other around, just a ten- by twenty-five-foot chain-link rectangle in the middle of a yard that was pretty in 1980 but had lost its charm as the years added up. The perennials had faded and died and were not replaced, the trees weren't trimmed, the grass wasn't fertilized, and the fence had been allowed to rot.

On moving day, I introduced them to their new home. They were not impressed, but went along with things; as long as we were near, they would follow us anywhere. I walked them every day. There was a pond nearby and our route circled it, spanning three and a half miles. I was in great shape, the dogs enjoyed it, and we tried to be happy.

But we weren't—we just couldn't admit it. Too much effort and heartbreak went into the move, not to mention too much money. Moving in 2006 was an expensive undertaking. Property values were sky high, realtor commissions correlated with the inflated prices, and real estate taxes went up with the property values. We were stuck. Or so I thought. Cheryl's condition deteriorated shortly after we moved, and what had seemed a promising new beginning became an ugly dead end. The house didn't work. That's when we packed up our stuff, I rolled up the pen, and we sold the bungalow and moved into Tara's family's old house.

Life is funny; all of your plans get thrown out the window as it progresses, and who you had envisioned yourself becoming turns out to be a completely different person when you get there. The man who moved into the rented house was a shell of the man who moved into his first home. I was cynical, tired, and simply depressed. Cheryl followed a similar path into disillusionment. The wheels of our life had fallen off, and it wasn't just the MS. Life in general had taken its toll on us as well, along with the realization that our dreams just might not be possible and what we had created might not be all it was cracked up to be.

We were the couple everybody wanted to be at one time, and it didn't seem that far away. But every day it slipped further from us, and we just couldn't reel it in.

I built a ten- by twenty-foot pen in the yard of the place we were renting and put their doghouses in a corner. We walked, and those walks were my only peaceful moments. The dogs, the sky, the breeze from Gaspee Point, and simple motions took the place of my frustration and angst, giving me a temporary reprieve from the doubt and dissatisfaction I had allowed to creep into my psyche.

Cheryl never even had that. She couldn't walk, couldn't escape the life that we had created, couldn't turn her back on the disillusionment or disappointment, and stayed in the house while I went to work, or walked the dogs. She was forced to stand on the sidelines as her life sped past. It wasn't fair, and it wasn't right, but it was what it was, and there wasn't a lot we could do about it.

I found a house a few blocks from where we were renting and showed Cheryl, who was less than impressed, but at that moment in our lives, she would have been less than impressed with a mansion. We put in an offer, bought it, and moved in. The dogs came with us. This time, there was no pen. They were old now, I figured, and I set up their doghouses in the yard where they could look in while living out. They would have the run of the yard, and the fence would give them all the boundaries they needed. They would be okay when I went to work for days at a time, I figured, and Cheryl could open the french doors from our dining room into the back yard and feed them. Everything would be hunky-dory, I figured.

I figured wrong. Way wrong. The dogs were older, and with age comes more need. They needed me, and I wasn't there. Our walks had become infrequent. One walk ended when Zimba had a seizure about a mile from home. I carried him home, and we put him on medication, but he had moments of strangeness where he would be dazed for a while, and sometimes he simply fell over. He had more good days than bad. Lakota was good, though—or as good as could be expected for an arthritic twelve-year-old Siberian husky living in the heat of Rhode Island in August.

They became estranged from us and wouldn't come when called, instead spending their days and nights stalking rabbits. A colony of them lived in our yard. Under the shed, in little rabbit bungalows, under the grass: I have no idea where else, because try as I might, I could never get rid of them, but the dogs were obsessed. They stopped coming to the french doors for their dinner and stayed up all night chasing ghosts in the yard. I worked my usual eighty-hour weeks, and Cheryl stayed home and tried to tell me about the situation, but I was full—full of myself—and unable to see that the situation at home was going downhill and gaining momentum as it went.

At three in the morning, on a sultry August night, the sound of crickets filling the foggy landscape and rabbits frolicking around the yard, a scream like I had never heard came from the yard. We immediately got up, Cheryl struggling to follow me to the door, and when we opened it, the dogs were nowhere to be found. I heard whimpering from afar, behind the shed, and walked over to it. The dogs walked away as one and went to the other side of the yard. I tried to get near them again, but they kept moving away when I got close.

"We'll figure it out in the morning," I said. Cheryl tried for a long time to get them to come, and I fell back asleep while they continued to ignore her calls. In the morning, I was able to track them down. Lakota was missing an eye. Wire garden fence had come loose and a twelve-inch length of stiff wire protruded from the fence. In the path of a running dog, it had landed perfectly and poked her eye out.

Zimba was beside himself, Lakota was in agony, Cheryl was in tears, and I was overcome with grief. It was as if the culmination of everything we had endured since our first move was upon us at that moment, and the realization that we were in trouble—big, real trouble—was so evident I couldn't believe I had not seen it before. I simply couldn't expect Cheryl to stay home alone and take care of the house, the dogs, me, and herself. It was too much. Way too much. I had to work, and I had to work overtime. Our lives were falling apart right before our eyes, and it took Lakota losing an eye for me to see it.

Our vet was closed. Our Plan B vet was closed. For an hour, we fretted and worried and tried to comfort Lakota, but she was inconsolable. Zimba was so upset that he became scary, and we didn't know what to do. But we had to do something.

We drove toward the emergency vet's office, a forty-five minute drive through a steady downpour, the dogs in the back seat of our Toyota Camry wagon, Lakota whimpering but somehow wagging her tail—she had always loved the car. Zimba watched over her. When we arrived at the office, we arrived at our decision: the dogs had to go. There was nobody to adopt a wolf-dog and a sick, one-eyed husky. Even if there were, the dogs' runs were nearly over. In a perfect world, they would have a year of life left before the inevitable end, six months more likely, and that time would be dreadful for everybody, especially the dogs.

We put them down. We had to. I keep telling myself that, and if I continue to do so I might just believe it. If I believe it, I just might forgive myself. I don't think the dogs forgive me, though. Six months to them is like four years to us, and they left us long before they were supposed to. And it was all my fault.

Cheryl and I were with them until the end, the four of us in a tiny exam room. Zimba and Lakota were lying at our feet, looking up at us as we cried. They were confident that we would make things better and were waiting to leave so they could get back to their rabbits. But the rabbits never came; the vet did. She injected them with some medication that relaxed them, and we held them as they became dazed. Then an IV was started, the doctor injected another syringe into their veins, and they died together, just like they had lived. They were gone, and Cheryl and I were alone.

We drove home and entered the house that our lives had built—the culmination of all of our efforts, the embodiment of our lives together. We went into separate rooms and wept. I could barely hear her sobbing from where I sat; the walls muffled the sound. I looked out the window into my empty backyard and truly believed the grief would kill me. And I secretly hoped that it would.

Chapter 40

FORGIVENESS

"He seems happy."

"We seem happy."

"Maybe it's contagious."

I looked at my wife, sitting happily on our patio for the first time since I could remember. The yard had not been a happy place and held some unpleasant memories.

"Maybe it is."

I reached for her hand and she took it, and Mr. Wilson went about his business, chasing moths, licking bark, climbing trees, and loving life.

"I'm sorry about the dogs," she said.

"Why are you sorry?"

"Because you lost them because of me."

"It was my fault, not yours."

"If I could have taken care of them while you were gone, we could have kept them."

"That's not your fault."

"It doesn't make it better."

"I should have built them a pen."

"I hated you for leaving them in the yard with no pen."

"I know."

But I never did build them a pen, and they paid the price, ultimately.

Mr. Wilson sauntered over to us, tilted his head and looked at Cheryl, then at me, then he laid on the cement, finally putting his head on the ground with a resounding *hrumph*.

"I guess he told us," I said.

"He does have a way with words," she smiled. We sat outside for a while, the three of us and the ghosts. But even they settled down after a while and watched the new dog play.

The day was chilly, and the promise of summer was in the air, but it was fleeting. The breeze blew out any warmth that managed to gather. It was nice to sit outside, and having a focus in the guise of a fuzzy white bundle of energy was refreshing. Eventually the chill in the air won: Cheryl went inside, and Mr. Wilson and I went for a walk. He was quickly becoming the Guardian; his job was keeping an eye on the neighborhood. We were the Neighborhood Watch during our time walking—he saw all, heard all, and investigated all. I had not seen the need to continue teaching him "heel," and let him push the limits of the extendable leash. He took all twenty feet and strained to go farther than the lead allowed every time a strange sight or sound happened. When cars or other people and their dogs approached, I said, "heel," and brought him and the leash in. He complained a little, and strained a little, but always came back.

Nick was shooting baskets, and he was alone.

"Hey, Nick," I greeted him.

"Hey."

Mr. Wilson exhibited thirty times more enthusiasm than the two of us combined and strained to get closer to our neighbor. He dragged me forward, and Nick put his ball down, crouched low, and tried to pet the goofy little critter who absolutely, positively had to say hello. Instead of sitting and allowing the human to pet him, he launched himself into Nick's arms, nearly knocking him over, and enthusiastically licked his face. Nick couldn't suppress his joy, and his smile lit up the neighborhood. He laughed and tried to keep hold of the squirmy little bugger, but found it difficult. As soon as Mr. Wilson's feet hit the ground, he was back in Nick's arms and the love fest continued.

"Traitor," I said, but felt a wonderful sense of gratitude as I watched the two play. A boy and his dog are a match made in heaven, and for the moment heaven was right in front of me. Nick was able to forget about his dying dad for a few minutes, and the break in grief did him a world of good. As Mr. Wilson and I walked away, we left a kid nailing three pointers and smiling; the boy missing layups and living in a world of grief and uncertainty went inside for a little while and rested.

It was a short but invigorating walk, and before long it was over. Nick had gone into his house, and Mr. Wilson and I went into ours. I thought of all the houses we passed during our walk and of all the secrets that live inside of them. To the casual passerby, Nick's is just another house on a street full of them, and nobody would ever know that a life-and-death struggle was going on inside the walls, and a boy was about to become a man without a father. How could they know when we spend so much time building our walls and work long hours keeping them secure?

"How's Nick?" asked Cheryl, when we entered the kitchen. Our kitchen sink has a window above it with a view of Nick and Dutch's house. She had seen us while cleaning up and was curious about the situation across the street. MS comes with its own set of walls, and those are tough to climb.

"Good as can be. Wilson seems fond of him."

Wilson busied himself swiffering around the cat's dishes, licking up crumbs.

"He's very sensitive."

"Nick?"

"No. Wilson."

Mr. Sensitive sat by the french doors, surveying his new kingdom, as birds descended upon our feeders and squirrels gathered around the base, picking up the dropped food.

Chapter 41

ABILITY TO SEE

Fascinated with our "Rescue Dog," we wanted to learn everything we could about others. Were they all as wonderful as Mr. Wilson? Did they show gratitude, obedience, creativity, and affection the way he did? Did they come with similar baggage: the heartbreaking body language of fear, the soulful expression in their eyes, the inability to hold their pee when certain people came too close to them? How did they become rescue dogs? How could we help?

Danielle, Brittany, and Eric had pitched in and bought us a Smart TV for Christmas. It sat in a box in our living room until March because neither one of us felt smart enough to hook it up. Eventually, I gathered my courage and opened the box and read the directions, then plugged it in, and it actually worked. It was difficult, time consuming, and took every ounce of resolve I had, but I did it. I plugged it in, and it worked. Then I followed the on-screen instructions and within five minutes we had an Internet-connected TV right in our bedroom. It was fabulous; we were able to watch our favorite shows, all of them on the major networks. None of them needed cable, satellite, or Smart TVs to come in clear as a bell. A simple pair of rabbit ears would do, but we had just entered a new dimension and, being Smart TV–armed, we were ready. We even subscribed to Netflix. Other than that, the smart features of the Smart TV sat idle. We are not the most tech-savvy people, and we used our expensive new toy like a simple old-fashioned television. But at least it we being used.

We were lying on our bed one day, a rare occasion—idle time at the Morse Mansion is normally spent doing tasks that Cheryl has deemed absolutely imperative—when I discovered Apps. The TV came with a YouTube app, and the fun began. I entered "dog rescue stories" in the search box, and seconds later dozens appeared on our screen. For hours we sat, tear-filled eyes fixed on the screen, and watched story after story of emotional dog rescues. There was Fiona, a blind homeless dog who had been living near a dumpster in a trash heap. She was 100 percent blind, and the people who rescued her got her to an appropriate veterinarian who restored her sight in one eye. It was truly a remarkable story, and we watched it over and over. There were stories involving what we learned are called "the Victory Dogs," the soldiers that fought in football star Michael Vick's illegal dogfighting ring. They were trained fighters turned loving pets, all through the love of humans who took the time to resurrect their innate goodness and let them be the dogs nature had intended them to be. Another story focused on a little hairy dirtball who ran away every time the rescuers came close, but was eventually captured and given a haircut and a bath. When she was done, she looked like she could be Mr. Wilson's sister! Sarah's beautiful "Angel" made the experience even better.

Mr. Wilson sat next to us, his eyes rapt with attention as his brethren's stories were told and the stories kept coming. It was incredibly moving, and when we had finally seen enough we all felt more connected to each other and more connected to the people who dedicate so much of their lives to helping homeless animals.

I had spent the previous twenty-two years working in the inner city, and seeing the worst of what people are capable of. The things people are capable of doing to each other are truly frightening. Shootings, stabbings, baseball-bat attacks, rapes, and robberies—the list is endless. With all the human suffering I saw as a firefighter and EMT, the suffering of helpless dogs and cats had taken a backseat. Seeing dogs abused and beaten and litters of puppies left in back stairways to die and worse, far worse, had become commonplace. When there are people shot or dying nearby, the images of those poor suffering animals needed to be forgotten before I could do my job.

I had lost my ability to see the possibilities before me. I had become a hard person, not oblivious to the suffering and neglect so many pets were enduring, but worse—seeing it and doing nothing to help.

I left that job when I couldn't do it anymore, and slowly my empathy is returning, as is my ability to dream what I once thought impossible. By doing a small part in a bigger scheme, I can help the plight of the animals I had once been forced to turn my back on. Because I cannot save them all doesn't mean I can't help one. Or two.

We adopted Wilson, not knowing who would turn up in that truck from Arkansas. Did we get lucky, or are all, or at least most, of the pets available for adoption as wonderful as he is? Of course they are! Each animal is its own miracle and has a lot to offer to anybody willing to accept the gifts they bring. My belief that the universe is a good place, a place where love reigns supreme, is reaffirmed every time I'm with Mr. Wilson. His place in the universe is right here with us, and if lying on the bed on a lazy Sunday afternoon is where we are, then that is exactly where we are supposed to be. I cannot turn back time and help the animals I had to leave behind, but here and now, in the moment, I can do my best to never do so again. Dogs live in the moment, I think, and from all I have read, they are incapable of remembering past events or worrying about the future.

Knowing this, and believing it for the most part, I can't stop myself from questioning the validity of their supposed inability to remember the past; for example, Mr. Wilson often shies away from me as if I were about to strike him. Fear was introduced to him by somebody, and he has to overcome that fear and trust that whatever happened to him is not going to happen again. This is simply an ugly, old emotion. Dogs may not have the ability to remember the way we humans understand memories, but hidden in their DNA is the knowledge that there is potential for pain every time there is interaction with a human. Lack of memory does not negate a dog's realization that humans can strike out with little or no warning and hurt them, and for them to fully trust their new owners is next to impossible. The fact that Mr. Wilson does so as much as he does is miraculous.

I wish I knew what happened to him to make him quiver when somebody raises their voice; he tries to shrink into the floor, not be seen, and become invisible. I wish I knew how to erase those emotions from him, let him fully appreciate the moment, and live his life knowing that nobody will hit him, or kick him, or toss him aside like an old rag, or tie him up in a freezing barn hungry, cold, alone, and surrounded by his own waste. But I can't. The only thing I can do, that any of us can do, is to never let it happen again.

Chapter 42

BREAD

"He's a piece of bread," said Cheryl one day, after Mr. Wilson did exactly what we expected him to do with no protest or dillydallying.

"He's a what?" I asked, having never heard this one before. Up to that point, I thought I had heard them all.

"He's a piece of fresh-baked bread, just out of the oven, still steaming, with a big blob of melting butter on it."

I could actually taste it, and it was sweet. Bread was a distant memory for Cheryl and me, having given up gluten, dairy, and sugar two years prior to adopting Mr. Wilson. We had read of the benefits of a diet that emphasized fresh fruits, vegetables, lean meat and fish, seaweed, radishes, and turnips. It's not as bad as it sounds, once you get used to it. According to Dr. Terry Wahls, from her book *The Wahls Protocol: How I Beat Progressive MS Using Paleo Principals and Functional Medicine*, a diet consisting of nine cups of colored vegetables, green vegetables, root vegetables, and fruit plus organic, grass-fed meats and certain kinds of fish will help cure multiple sclerosis. That, and the neuroelectrical stimulation we did every chance we got, will lead us into a healthy future and walking will be a breeze. We do the diet and the e-stim because nobody has any better ideas. Cheryl is getting better, though, and the groundwork for healing is in place. When it is time for her body to repair the damage done to her central nervous system and start walking normally, we will be ready.

"I'd eat him if he were a piece of bread."

"I'd eat your arm if it were a piece of bread."

"I'd sell the house for a piece of bread."

"I'd sell you for a piece of bread."

And when we were through fantasizing about bread, we finished our kale salad. But we did have some cheese to top it off. Cheese made with cashews, nutritional yeast, salt, and a tablespoon of lemon, that is. It's actually pretty good.

Life with Mr. Wilson became routine, and it was as though we never lived our lives without him in it. He simply was. He slept with us, walked with us, exercised with us, and even came to work with us. He liked that part of his routine, even though the best part for him was the moment he realized that we were taking him with us when we left the house. I often wonder what our pets think we do when we leave them alone in the house, or if they even miss us. My guess is they do. Judging from the reception we get from Mr. Wilson when we return, he notices we are missing more than the cats do—those erstwhile creatures who linger around the edges of our space, entering when they are hungry or when we are troubled. Say what you will about the aloof nature of the feline species, but I live with their idiosyncrasies and have experienced their talent for knowing exactly when their presence is needed the most.

As my career as a firefighter ebbed, the next chapter of our lives began in earnest. Cheryl liked to "go tanning," as we like to say here in Rhode Island. The place that she "went tanning" was going out of business—a result of poor management.

Selling something that you can get for free six months out of the year is a challenge in the best of times—selling sunshine in a recession a bit more daunting. But somehow we did it. We bought the defunct tanning salon where Cheryl once spent money, and now we make money offering the best possible experience for people who enjoy what we offer. Our philosophy in all things is to simply do the absolute best of which you are capable and, by doing so, success will follow. Success is not measured by monetary reward, thankfully; SUNKissT TANS is no juggernaut of industry, but we operate a small business in a difficult place to do business and we offer a product that is relentlessly attacked for various reasons beyond our control.

Mr. Wilson loves the place. When it's time to go to work, he gets all jacked up—as we like to call his behavior when something good is going to happen—his anticipation palpable as he glues himself to one of us and can barely contain his excitement when the tell-tale signs of departure appear. The shoes going on results in a cock of his head, rummaging around for whatever last-minute things we need at work gets him on his feet, picking the keys off the keyholder sends him into a spiral, and taking his leash from the wall next to the garage door is enough to send him into orbit.

We bought a car seat for him after his second ride in the car resulted in vomit, and he took to it well. He sits a foot above the back seat, nestled in his little basket looking like a king on his throne. He is latched to the seat and has very limited mobility, but he doesn't mind a bit and looks out the window as we drive through our town. It's a short ride, and before long we're there, and he is in his spot behind the counter, waiting for his subjects to enter and pay him homage before going off to the back, where they bathe themselves in bright light for a while, then come back, a little more colorful and always a lot happier.

He has no way of knowing what it is these people do, but he knows that this is a happy place, and he's content to be part of it, even if that means he is confined to a five- by five-foot area. The customers either love him or ignore him, and either is fine with him. He holds no grudges and harbors no resentment. He simply knows who will appreciate him and he responds likewise to the friendly gestures from the strangers who visit.

A dog needs purpose, and getting Mr. Wilson out of the house and into the work world does him a world of good. Lying around all day waiting for slaves to bring food is no way to live, for a king or a dog, and the stimulation new people bring in the form of scent, aura, and sounds is invaluable. He is better for it, and so are we. The customers like it, too.

Along with the herding dogs, hunting dogs, guard dogs, rescue dogs, abused rescue dogs, and working dogs, we now have the first of a new category of dog—the ambassador dog who does it all.

Chapter 43

GOODNIGHT, DUTCH

I hadn't seen Dutch for days. The house was quiet; even Nick stayed inside. At one point, people showed up. Just like that, there they were. It wouldn't be long now, I figured. The wagons were circled: cars from different states, people from different states, most of whom I've never seen, converged on my Dutch's house to be with him when he died. I couldn't believe how fast it all happened; it seemed like only yesterday he was a huge part of the neighborhood—big, robust, and full of life. I used to see him every day. He was part of my life, a small but important part of the everyday, comfortable flow: the wave in the morning as I drove off to work, the hello's on rubbish night, helping the other neighbors when the snow drifts piled high in winter, helping each other when our snow throwers broke down.

I'm on the outside now, as people from his past take precedence—his estranged wife, a brother I never knew he had, sons from a previous marriage who I knew he looked forward to visiting once a year, one in Vegas, the other in Virginia. It has to be this way, and I know that; family matters at the end and neighbors slink off into the background. I was glad we had yesterday, when I stopped by looking to borrow a drill so I could erect a dividing wall to keep Mr. Wilson out of the family room and off the new rug he had become fond of peeing on. I gave him a pass because the rug is green and he's a dog . . . And what the heck, nobody is perfect and I never liked that color anyway.

I had been in Dutch's house for a few minutes when suddenly a white streak came bounding through the garage, into the kitchen—we had left the door open—onto Dutch's recliner, and into his lap. Dutch laughed, a dry, brittle laugh, but one with all the joy he could muster. We visited for a little while, and I knew the end was near, but didn't know just how near. Nick joined us, and Mr. Wilson gave him the attention he needed. We went back home, but only after getting a baby gate from the attic, which Dutch insisted I take with me. He was that way until the end— offering his antique hutch that he kept in his garage to me and wanting me to come back and take that too.

"Don't go giving all of your stuff away just yet," I said, and Mr. Wilson said nothing but goodbye.

I looked out of my kitchen window a few hours later and saw an oxygen delivery truck rolling away, and then another car and a nurse to go with it. I knew the morphine would be coming soon, and his respirations would slow, and his breathing would get shallow, and then it would all stop.

At ten than night, people stood outside his garage, some smoking, some drinking, all lost, strangers to each other, dealing with a loss nobody saw coming and wondering if they could have done more to bridge the gaps that widen as days turn to months, and months to years, and communication slows and then stops.

Then there's a call nobody wants, with the cryptic words, "come soon, we don't have much time."

I don't think it will be long before his house is empty, and Nick will be gone. I'll look over there every day and wave to the ghost across the street. Wilson will look over there, too, and wonder where everybody went, but he will feel no grief or loss. He'll continue on his path, befriending everybody who he feels is worthy. The exuberance that he shows is remarkable, but it is not for everybody. Something happened in his past that keeps him from fully trusting everybody on sight. There must be some cloudy memories of pain in that little head of his, and certain people, through no fault of their own, bring those emotions to the forefront. He doesn't lash out at people who intimidate him; rather, he cowers and worries, but ultimately gets close enough for them to be touched by him.

I'm glad Dutch and Nick got to meet him, and it makes me happy there was no reticence or fear on his part and that he gave them what little joy could be squeezed from the dark days that existed for them over the last few months. There is something everlasting about the spirit that accompanies a dog, something that, as smart as we are, we will never fully understand. We have the brains and reasoning ability to know everything, but what do we really know? Perhaps there is a completely different way of communicating that we cannot comprehend, something that far surpasses our ability to understand the world around us and the people in our lives. Maybe each species is gifted with senses that surpass what we think are the five biggies—sight, hearing, smell, taste, and touch. Our eyes see, our ears hear, and our noses smell things. Our tongues taste and our skin feels, but is that all there is? We feel emotions like love, fear, and hate, and sense those feelings in others, but how deeply? Is a dog able to sense those emotions as clearly as we can see written words on a page or hear the crescendo as our favorite songs reach their climactic peak?

I think so. I think they are capable of that, as well as things that we cannot imagine. In their bodies, which are vastly different from ours, I think that they, too, know when they are needed most and are able to make their feelings known with absolute clarity. For those fortunate enough to be on the receiving end of a dog's attention, the result is one of the things that makes the mysteries of living not only bearable, but incredible.

Chapter 44

BACK TO THE BEACH

"You want to take Mr. Wilson to the beach?" Cheryl asked. We had been hanging around the house doing busy work, it was a beautiful day, and the beach would be perfect. But what beach? My beach, the place Cheryl had only visited once, the place where I sort out my demons, or some other beach? Perhaps a new beach with new possibilities, or better yet—an old beach with new possibilities.

Though we lived only a few miles from the very same Conimicut Point where two people shared their dreams and desires while sitting atop a lifeguard chair—right above the "Stay Off!" sign—all those years ago, we never went there. Cheryl would sometimes drive there to be alone—it was a beautiful place, and close—but the magic had left when our relationship soured.

"Conimicut Point?" I asked, anxiously.

She smiled. I got the leash.

We knew we were in love, and that we had never stopped being in love. We just needed somebody to remind us. Mr. Wilson sat in the back seat of our car, in his perch, and watched the world go by as we drove toward the shore. The sun seekers had left for the day, leaving room for the folks who wanted nothing more than a few moments near the sea, where life moves a little slower and problems don't seem as difficult to solve. We parked the car in a handicapped spot, exchanged dirty looks with the old man in the car sitting next to us, and put the placard on the rearview mirror. He wouldn't be satisfied with that, though; he needed to see real disability before he would look the other way. I used to get annoyed with the attention and take it personally, but that was before I had let the reality of Cheryl's hardships sink in. On some level, I knew she was disabled, I just wouldn't admit it. Other people could look all they wanted and question Cheryl's validity, it didn't matter. What mattered was us.

I stepped out of the car and into the essence of the beach. Just being in the parking lot is close enough to feel it and know that you have returned to the place you belong. I was grateful Cheryl suggested we come and tried my hardest to enjoy the moment, but moments from my years as a firefighter crept into my unconscious mind and clouded my reality. Twenty-two years is a long time to spend with the dead and dying, and some images simply refuse to be expunged. Even the fresh air and salt water couldn't completely remove the melancholy from me.

Seagulls flew past, soaring high above us, their bills full of clams, crabs, and mussels picked from the water's edge. Birds have to eat, I figured, but why do clams have to die? Waves broke near the water's edge, and children and a few adults chased them, frolicking in the cool water as the tide marched relentlessly toward land. Low tide had reached its peak, and the sand bar that extended from land to a lighthouse a few hundred yards offshore was swallowed by the bay. The land bridge was simply no more. It came back every day, though, and people ignored the riptide and undertow warnings and wandered as far as they could go to dip their feet into the tumultuous water at the edge of land. It looked innocent enough, but every year an unsuspecting person or two would be lost when the tide quickly devoured the sand. They underestimated their ability to conquer the immense power of the ocean. Their bodies would be twisted, and they would sink and drown. More times than not, a would-be rescuer would drown right along with them, and their bodies would wash ashore when the water decided it was time to give them up. It happened a day earlier, when a sixteen-year-old kid from Providence was swept away, his body found hours later.

I pushed the dreary images aside and helped Cheryl step out of the car. We opened the rear door: I got Mr. Wilson, Cheryl got her cane, and the old bastard that had looked upon us with disdain until confirming my wife's level of disability to be adequate returned to his newspaper. People milled about the parking lot. A group of men smoked cigarettes and drank coffee while discussing the events of the day. They said hello as we walked past them, offering uncomfortable glances and sneaky stares as a beautiful woman limped past them, her cane so out of place but impossible to ignore. I held Cheryl's right hand while she navigated the uneven surface with the cane in her left. Mr. Wilson scooted ahead of us, straining at the end of the leash, anxious to get to the water.

We got close, settling for a bench at the end of the beach grass, about a hundred feet from the water. Mr. Wilson fretted for a while, but eventually settled down. Our lifeguard chair, or more likely the fifth or sixth incarnation of ours, had been moved to a different part of the beach. The area where it had been was closed to swimmers because of high levels of pollution in the water. A sign was stuck into the sand, driven deep enough so the tides and vandals could not budge it. The area to the left of the sign was polluted, to the right was not. It was okay, though; when we were younger, the entire area was polluted and there were no signs telling us not to swim there—just a lot of dead fish.

It's funny how I see things differently now. Twenty-two years of firefighting and all that came with it took a big piece of my soul. They call it PTSD, and I never knew I had it until I left the job and started living again.

I held Cheryl close and forgot about the dead fish, the disappearing sand bar, drowned teenagers, and shellfish, and closed my eyes. I felt our dog tugging on his leash and remembered how it felt to sit on a lifeguard chair at midnight with the girl I loved.

Chapter 45

ARKANSAS

As good as it is having Mr. Wilson in our lives, old habits die hard, old routines sneak up on you, and before you know it, everything is taken for granted. A dog can only do so much, even a dog as great as Mr. Wilson. It took a long time for my and Cheryl's relationship to sour, and it wasn't going to be fixed overnight. Things did begin to get better as soon as we picked up Mr. Wilson from the highway rest stop, but our lives are a journey, and the relationships we forge as the trip moves on are part of that roller-coaster ride we call life. Peace and tranquility are obtainable, and I'm certain we will obtain it eventually, but I'm in no rush for the journey to end.

Some days are just better than others, and the bad ones must be endured so the good ones can be fully appreciated. The chemistry that exists between people in long-term relationships goes buggy every now and then, and there is precious little we can do to stop it or turn it around. Sometimes an outside influence is needed, and every now and then one comes through.

He senses when we are not right, and then he is not right. If we are feeling the slightest bit of tension or anger or sadness, our feelings are absorbed by him and he responds accordingly. When there is tension in the air, his body language communicates it vividly. The weight of the world becomes his, and it crushes his spirit. He backs away and retreats to his safe place. It breaks my heart to see, so I try and look happy, but he isn't fooled, so I make myself happy, and then he is happy, too.

I actually saw him cry once, and it was the saddest thing I had ever seen. The sight was enough to make me stop everything; my thoughts, my actions, my racing mind. I controlled my breathing and sat with him. I rubbed the tear from his eye and let him know that sometimes tears are good, but tears are for men, women, children, and often babies . . . not for dogs.

"We'll do the crying around here, Mr. Wilson," I told him, and we lay next to him on the bed. He rubbed his paws over his eyes and looked at us like we were the king and queen of the world and actually could make tears disappear forever. He looked at us, first Cheryl, then me, and his eyes begged us to quit it and make it like it was before so we could be happy again. The phone rang, and he cocked his head the way he does and grinned.

"Hey y'all, it's Cheri, from Arkansas!"

Cheryl's face lit up and my body relaxed, and Mr. Wilson put his head on the bed, closed his eyes, and listened as Cheryl put our caller on speakerphone.

"Wilson misses you," said Cheryl.

"I miss him, too," said Cheri, her Southern charm and accent exactly what we needed. "Is he okay?"

"He's truly a great dog. If God were to get the baby Jesus a puppy, he would have gotten him Wilson," Cheryl replied.

A great Southern laugh filled our room and the tinny sound from the speaker managed to sound like a PA system when it did.

"I told you he was special! He just loves you up! I miss that little man, and so does Tippy. I swear, Tippy is a better dog because of Wilson. He was a scared little thing before Wilson showed him how to live. He plays now, and runs through the yard like him and Wilson used to do, and he snuggles right up with me when I sit and watch TV. He even sleeps with me now."

"Did you adopt Tippy?" Cheryl asked.

"Me and Mama had a big ol' beautiful dog, and then she had some pups and we had them, but they died after twenty years. I didn't have a dog, but one day Mama showed up and sure enough the cutest little thing was with her. She got him from the pound, a little Yorkie, but he was all scared and shy, but we love him and he kept us company out here. We live way out in the country on five acres. Mama's got a double-wide and she likes it okay, but I need my space and I live in a twelve by eighteen-foot room near her 'cause she gets scared at night and I like to be close—but not too close."

"Wow," said Cheryl. It sounded nice out there.

We had wondered about Cheri's home. She had mentioned that she lived in a twelve-foot house, but we couldn't imagine it.

"It's cozy, and it's mine," she said through the phone lines. "It's got a microwave and a little stove and a five-foot refrigerator. Got a washroom too but no shower but it suits me fine. Outside, me and Mama sit on our porch and watch the critters; we got lots of critters, deer, and I saw a pretty red fox today on the side of the road. He must have been hit by a car 'cause he was all dazed, and his tail was longer than he was, but he just stood there lookin' at me. I took a picture, then he shook it off like a cat that gets hit does and he ran off into the woods."

Cheryl and I sat on our bed, rapt attention on the voice coming from a different world, a simple place where simple things are appreciated. The tension was gone, love had returned, and we listened as Cheri talked about her life.

"We have a Wal-mart. It's nine miles from us, but it's not so far. Got us some sugar water and hummingbird feeders, and me and Mama put on our red T-shirts and fill those feeders up and then we watch the hummingbirds feed, it's really something to see. We had maybe a few, then a few more, and now we have a hundred and forty of 'em eating at our feeders. One of 'em got stuck, have you ever seen a hummingbird feeder?"

"We have the same one here," said Cheryl. "We bought it at Wal-mart."

"Then you know what happened: the little hummingbird was feeding and then a bunch more tried to take his place when he moved, and he got stuck between the feeder and the perch. Poor little thing couldn't free himself, so I went over and I put my finger and thumb around his little body and I wiggled him free. I said, 'Mama, you gotta see this 'cause you'll never see anything like it again,' and I showed her the bird before he flew away."

We talked for a while and made tentative plans to visit, and she offered her home to us and told us about her neighbors and how they all raise cattle, but seldom do much with them. They do get a tax break from having them, and she would cook me a great big T-bone steak, and if that didn't do it, she'd cook me another! We would have sweet corn and potatoes, and look at her garden. She had planted watermelon and tomatoes and some beans, and we were welcome to all of it.

Eventually she had to get back to work, and we said our goodbyes. We all felt better having connected. Dinner was good that night, and we ate in bed with dishtowels for table cloths and had hamburgers that tasted like T-bone steaks. Mr. Wilson had three cookies, and he was happy. And so were we.

PART III: THE FUTURE

Chapter 46

PURPOSE

I never knew how much I missed having a dog in my life. A dog gives the day purpose; caring for somebody who truly needs to be cared for makes getting up in the morning about more than brushing my teeth, sating my hunger, and going off to work. The routine that includes taking care of Mr. Wilson becomes a natural part of the day: feeding him, letting him out, playing with him a little, and having him close. His is a comforting presence in our home, and we are truly fortunate to have him.

Because of him, Cheryl and I have been exposed to a world that we had only been on the fringes of, having never fully embraced the meaning and importance of rescuing homeless pets. Most of the dogs and cats that became giant parts of our life were obtained from shelters or just happened upon us, but we never truly understood the enormity of the problem. It's not all about the pet, we have learned. The pet is the catalyst, the people the beneficiaries.

Each stage of the adoption process has the potential to fill a void in a person's life. There are people who volunteer their time by inspecting the homes of prospective adopters, people with the means to write checks, and people with time to spend at the local animal shelters or donate food and other necessities to the many animal rescue groups. There are people who squeak out a living transporting homeless pets from where they are unwanted to places where they are wanted. There are people who cannot keep a dog in their home for good, but are able to foster one or more until permanent homes for them can be found. People write letters and run websites telling the stories and capturing the attention of people willing to listen. Then, there are people like us; people who wanted to get a dog, figured they would look into adopting, and not only found a dog who needed a home, but also found an entire world of people who devote their time and part or all of their lives helping the pets who cannot help themselves.

I used to firmly believe animal welfare was secondary to people's well-being, and still do to some extent, but I have learned that the two are intricately entwined. A person's well-being is positively affected by their relationship with an animal, and in our case, a dog. The improvement in our lives since Mr. Wilson came into them is profound, and a big surprise. It is difficult now for me to envision a dog-less life. So much of our time is spent doing things with him, for him, and because of him that it leads us to wonder what we did without him.

Just one of the many beautiful parts of all this is seeing a dog's life through different eyes. My old eyes were blind and didn't fully comprehend exactly what a dog in our lives meant. Perhaps the cycle of life with its ever-changing perception of our own reality is responsible for the message being blocked; in my youth, a dog was a good companion now and then, but was mostly a chore. There was simply too much going on in my life for the dog to be part of it. I guess that was okay with the dogs; they take things in stride and live for the moment. But I think I missed out on a lot of what a dog could offer, and more importantly, what I could offer a dog.

As life goes on, our needs change. Time—good, peaceful, and contented time—becomes more important than the rewards gained from expending it pursuing things that at the moment seem imperative. Then an understanding of what is essential becomes clear. Simply living—taking one breath, one step, and one moment at a time—is a skill learned when there is less time on top of the hourglass and more on the bottom. Appreciating the perfect simplicity that exists in a dog's mind—and knowing that time spent with him doing nothing more than basking in the glow of each other's company is perfect—is an important lesson and a gift that for some of us humans comes with a big price tag.

I have had great dogs in my life but was too young or distracted to appreciate them. There was Pete, a great German shepherd who I barely remember, but according to family legend bit me gently but firmly and was given away. We had a Collie named Lad, the male version of Lassie who was the all-American dog during the sixties. He was a good boy and a great fence climber. One day he climbed the fence that kept him enclosed in our yard and he never came back. We had a toy French poodle named Michelle. Hers was the life of luxury, eating and sleeping and watching her family grow during her short time with us. She made it to seven, when the German shepherd next door chased her down and mortally wounded her.

Then there was Shannon. One of the biggest regrets in my life is the way I treated her. She was the family dog, but our family had moved on: my brother Bob was away with the National Guard, and my sister Susan had joined the Army and was deployed to Germany, where she started a family of her own. Little Melanie was still at home, but she was a teenager who didn't have time to take care of Shannon, and my parents decided that they didn't either. I was living in what my dad affectionately called "White Harlem," a rundown three-bedroom apartment located behind a busy nightclub, and somehow ended up as Shannon's caretaker.

I did a lousy job of taking care of her. A twenty-year-old who drank too much and could barely take care of himself has no business taking care of a dog, and though I tried to do the best I could, I failed miserably. It was a dark time in my life—the high school party was over, and any of my friends with more than half a brain were away at college and the other half were busy destroying the half a brain we had left. I spent far too much time alone, living in a crummy house with no money, a girlfriend who went off to college and never came back, and friends of convenience who left as soon as the beer was gone. Shannon never complained when she went a day without food—she knew that beer was more important—and she remained loyal, never realizing her life should have been better. Eventually I realized that I had to let her go, and she ended up with a family who could take care of her properly, and had lots of land. She was able to run free, and had plenty of food and love. Sometimes life's lessons are taught at somebody else's expense, and learning how to take care of an animal or knowing when you can't was a difficult lesson to learn. Difficult for me, more so for Shannon. She would have stayed by my side no matter what, and I barely noticed.

If I could do it over again, I'd spend less time chasing my life and more time living it. And I might even spend a little more time chasing my dog around the yard or letting her chase me.

Nobody has to teach Mr. Wilson that game. He's known it all along. We ran through the yard, him chasing me, me chasing him, his ears flapping as he ran, expending every ounce of energy he had in him in every movement he made and resting when we were through. It is too late for Shannon, and I am ashamed of the way I treated her, but in some way I hope to make it up to her by being the best possible caretaker for Mr. Wilson.

Chapter 47

KARMA

A man needs food to survive, and thankfully there are places where food is available in such abundance and variety it boggles my mind. Today's hunter-gatherers have it made. Instead of leaving the village to go on a hunt and coming home days later, exhausted, dirty, and likely bleeding and scarred, we drive to the market and forage around the shelves for a little while, filling our baskets with fresh fruit, produce, fish, and meat. And we can even rent a movie from said market now and then.

I'm great at bringing things home from the market; it's bringing the movies back where I have difficulty. I swear, the movie rental people who live in those little red boxes outside the supermarket know how to make their product invisible once it is safely in the home of the consumer. Return trips to the market to return a forgotten movie are commonplace for me, and while there I see no reason not to forage for more food, because one never knows when the markets will run dry.

As Cheryl's disease progressed, my trips to the supermarket increased. I've actually gotten pretty good at it and have been known to clip a coupon or two while scanning the flyers from the three competing places that serve our area. More times than not, those coupons remain forgotten in my pocket, but if there is one thing I've learned, it's that I am a work-in-progress, and I am a long way from my ultimate goal of perfection.

"We need food," said Cheryl, after assessing the emptiness of our refrigerator, and off I went.

I hadn't traveled far when I realized I forgot the movie we had rented a few days ago. A decision had to be made. I calculated the distance from me to my house and the distance to the store where the little red box sits and decided that going home and getting it rather than paying the late fee was prudent. It frightens me that my mind actually works like that. Any normal man would simple turn the car around and go get the movie, or better yet, not forget it in the first place. Not me; that would be too simple.

Though I forgot the DVD itself, I did not forget the movie and the message it conveyed. Abandoned dogs could be united with people who had abandoned themselves, then trained and united with people who had been abandoned by society. It's such a simple concept, and one that would never have occurred to me had I not rented the movie, and I never would have rented the movie had we not adopted Mr. Wilson. And had we not rented the movie, and watched it together, with our new dog sleeping comfortably between us—both of us taking turns stroking his hair while he slept—we would not have realized while doing so that we were content, truly content, and happy to be together and sharing the same bed, the same moment, and the same love that had reentered our home. I had forgotten how good it felt to have somebody close, both physically and more importantly mentally, and to be comfortable together.

I turned the car around, retraced my path, snuck into the house, and put the movie into my back pocket with only Mr. Wilson knowing I had forgotten it in the first place. I may be able to cover my tracks and not let the Mrs. know that I'm losing my memory, but old Mr. Wilson is a tough dog to get one over on. Cheryl tells me that he camps at a window where he has the best view and waits for me to come home. He hears the car before he sees it, and he cocks his head, listening until I come into view. When he is certain it is me, he runs for the door and waits. I was oblivious to all of this and had no idea that this little creature actually cared so much. When I open the door, he goes nuts, and walks backward for ten or fifteen feet, then runs toward me, full of exuberance, and gives me the greatest greeting imaginable. He does it whether I'm gone for a day or a minute. I felt bad leaving so quickly, but the store waited.

I parked the car and approached the doorway to the super-market, passing mothers with carts full and kids following, an elderly woman struggling with her bundles, and some college kids who walked right past her. I considered offering my assistance to the older woman, and would have, but she made it to her car, an old Buick Park Avenue, before I could. She quickly opened the door and put her groceries down. It was probably better that way; these days an offer of help from a stranger is often considered suspicious, and I didn't want to scare the lady.

An attractive woman sat at a table to the right of the entrance doors, collecting money for something or other, so I instinctively steered myself as far away from the table as I could. My peripheral vision was sharp, however, especially when an attractive woman is within eyesight, and I also noticed that she had a big bucket of candy on her left and a big bucket of dollars on her right. In the middle of the table, perched in front of her, was a poster starring two schnoodles. The dogs in the photographs were okay, as far as schnoodles go, but not nearly as handsome as Mr. Wilson. Intrigued, I slowed my pace and glanced at the lady. I figured a buck wouldn't kill me.

"Are you raising money for schnoodles?" I asked, innocently enough. Another man was hovering around the table, pretending to be interested in the plight of the schnoodle while leering at the woman and not even glancing at the poster.

"In a way," she replied, grateful for the distraction. "It's the Providence Animal Rescue League's Twenty-fifth Annual Pet Walk."

"That's nice," I said, feigning interest. The other guy closed in, making some ridiculous remark about how much money he could raise. I gave him a dubious look and made some equally ridiculous comment about the dogs in the picture being cute, but not nearly as cute as the person raising money for them. Men. Give us a pretty lady to fight about, even if we both have pretty ladies at home and no intention of bringing home another one, and we simply cannot help acting like asses.

The lady quickly lost interest in both of us. Defeated, we glared at each other and went our separate ways; the other guy simply walked away while I put a buck into the bucket, searched the other bucket for gluten- and sugar-free chocolate, gave the lady a goofy grin, and walked into the store.

Ten minutes later, with a few bags of groceries in hand, I walked past the folding table again, smiled again, was ignored again, and kept on trucking. The groceries fit in the passenger seat—no need to open the trunk—and I leaned in and put them down. Then I sat on my rented copy of the movie *Shelter Me*, which had remained in my back pocket during my entire shopping spree.

Sometimes the simplest task becomes a giant chore. Returning a movie should be an easy thing, but if I had a nickel for every late charge I have paid because a movie stayed in my car or pocket, I'd have a lot of nickels.

Back to the big red box and past the pretty lady at the folding table.

"This was a good movie," I said to her before putting it into the slot. Those things amaze me. How does a machine know how to grab the thing and put it back into its rightful place? Little people inside? Probably not. Weird how things work and I have no clue how.

She was a little hesitant to engage me in conversation, but decided I was harmless and graced me with a slight smile and inquired about it.

"It's about shelter dogs, and inmates, and soldiers and people and second chances."

"Sounds like a winner. Do you have a dog?"

"I do. A schnoodle."

Her look was priceless, a mixture of contempt, amusement, revulsion, and disbelief. I took a few pamphlets, grinned a little more, mumbled something about karma, and went home.

Chapter 48

WALKING WITH DOGS

"Cheryl, look at this," I said, leaving the groceries on the kitchen counter. She took the pamphlet and scanned it for a moment, then handed it back to me.

"What about it?"

"It's a pet walk to help the homeless animals at the Providence Animal Rescue League. I was thinking maybe we could do it."

"I can't walk very far."

"That does make it hard to do a walk-a-thon. But you don't have to walk the whole thing; we can just say you did."

"That's lying."

"Just a little. But I'll do it, and Mr. Wilson will too, and you can be there and be the behind-the-scenes person."

"I don't want to be the behind-the-scenes person."

Who would? Sometimes the courage needed to take charge and make headlines pales in comparison to being the unheralded

"behind-the-scenes" person, living life unknown and misunder-
stood. A quiet, lonely resolve is needed to get up each day and face
the world on unsteady footing, firmly entrenching yourself in a
world that moves past you without a glance backward. Motion is
easy; it's taken for granted and gets all the accolades. It is the lack
of movement and the roots that stillness creates that allow the
foundation to grow stronger.

"You don't have a choice."

"No, I guess I don't."

She was sad, but intrigued. Living life on the sidelines after
being not only in the game, but running it for so long, is hard on
her. Watching people taking their legs for granted wears a person
down when they have a hard time walking to the bathroom, and
Cheryl's once remarkably resilient spirit had been showing signs
of weakness. But she took the pamphlet, read it, and decided
that we would not only do the thing, but we would also get the
people at our business involved. She got to work creating a spon-
sorship program and instituted the first annual "Win a Tanning
Package by Helping us Help Them" program. We spent the next
few hours running ideas back and forth. It was like the old days,
when conversation flowed freely and anything was possible. We
decided to create a "pack"—a group of people to raise funds—
that would enlist the help of Danielle and Brittany and the
people who worked at the tanning salon. Each of us would get
our own sponsors, and our goal was to raise five hundred dollars
for the cause.

"Have you considered the logistics of walking Mr. Wilson with
hundreds of dogs?" asked Cheryl.

"Considered the logistics? I don't even know what that means."

"He hasn't learned how to heel properly, or walk without
pulling, or do much of anything other than sit."

"Yeah, but in general he's pretty good."

"Pretty good? He could be great. He learns fast. Watch this," said Cheryl. "Wilson, come."

And he came.

"Wilson, sit."

And he sat.

"Big deal, I can do that."

Cheryl put one of his favorite cookies five feet in front of him on the floor. He began walking toward it. Cheryl put up her hand in a perfect traffic cop way and said, "stay."

He stayed.

"Wilson, sit."

He sat. He sat for a good thirty seconds. He sat so long I almost ate the cookie; it was just sitting there waiting to be devoured.

"Okay!" she said in a fun, engaging voice, and Mr. Wilson ran toward his bounty and gobbled it up. I was amazed, humbled, shocked, and in awe of my beautiful wife and her perfectly trained companion.

"How did you do that?" I asked.

"YouTube."

"Get out of here! You taught him to watch YouTube?"

"Honest, they have all sorts of videos that teach people how to train dogs. Some are really bad—you have to sift through a lot of baloney to get to the good ones, but one guy in particular is excellent."

"Who?"

"Zak George."

We spent the next couple of hours watching Zak on our swanky new Smart TV. Mr. Wilson watched, too. Even the cats got in on the party. It was quite a scene, a big galoot on one side of the bed, a tiny beautiful Italian lady on the other, and three critters in the middle. Zak made the training seem like fun, and I couldn't wait to get started. All I really thought I wanted was for Mr. Wilson to not pull on the leash when I walked him, but suddenly, through the magic of YouTube and Zak George, a whole world of animal training became not only a possibility, but something that I truly wanted to try.

My philosophy that dogs are better off doing what comes natural to them took a serious beating after just a few short film clips, and I learned that happy, content dogs need a whole lot more. They look up to us, their masters, and do not think about things like leadership and submission, Type A personalities, or ego—they just like to be comfortable in their own skin. Having a human who is confident and willing to let them learn new tricks is exactly what they like, and they look forward to challenges and success. It is essential to their development to be challenged, to excel, and to be praised. My reticence to be in control of another living being worked for Zimba, who was just wild enough to appreciate his independent status, but not as well for poor little Lakota, who had to take charge of her environment or be bullied by the big dumb wolf whom she shared her life with. Mr. Wilson craved leadership and wanted badly to make his leaders happy. It didn't make him a coward, or a wimpy little ankle biter; it made him true to himself and true to his true calling. I didn't create dogs, but whoever did made them thrive when performing tasks for their leaders. Once I figured that out, things got a lot better for everybody.

Cheryl was weeks ahead of me in the training department; while I was off in never-never land, she was busy learning how to get Mr. Wilson to listen. I thought it was kind of cool how he would sit for her and wait to have his dinner until she released him and how he didn't jump up on her when she came home. It was me who got all of the attention and love; me, the alpha male. It was obvious I was the big cheese, the head honcho, the imperial leader, and the boss. Mr. Wilson lived for the moments that he and I could be together, and he went ballistic when I left him. He had eyes only for me, and that was the way it had to be, because I, after all, was the Supreme Being.

"He doesn't respect you," said Cheryl one day, after my tenth try at getting my subject to stop jumping on me.

"Nonsense, I am the Supreme Being."

"He thinks you are his equal."

"Does not." Brilliant, I know, and certainly not worthy of a Supreme Being, but it was the best I could do with my worshipper trying his best to melt into me.

Chapter 49

WHO IS THE ALPHA?

I left my subjects at home and drove to the tanning salon. I like it there; it's a good place to get away from it all, put my mind on automatic pilot and not have to worry about anything except running the business. People come, people go, and we have nice conversations or we don't, depending on their mood when they come in. I have learned to let people talk about themselves when they stop in—it is, after all, their money they are spending in my place, and they do not need to hear about my problems. Elaine, the manager of our tanning salon and long-time friend, was gracious enough to point this out to me one day when I had been rambling on to a customer about something that somebody did that annoyed me. That customer may or may not come back.

Sometimes I forget my own rules, and when certain customers come in, I can't help myself. One of our favorite tanning customers, Christine, trains dogs for a living and is very well spoken on the subject. I've listened to her numerous times when she describes the people who bring their dogs to the place she works and the mistakes they make. On this occasion, I smiled knowingly as she vented, because I knew what she knew. I knew that I had what it took to be the leader of the pack, the Alpha Male and the boss.

I told her about my crazy wife, and her theory that Mr. Wilson thought he was my pal and not his master. Smugly, I carried on about how he charges me when he sees me and lavishes me with love, takes his leash and drags it to me, and runs out the door in anticipation of our walks together.

"It's so obvious that I'm the boss," I said, shaking my head in dismay.

"Well," she began, and I know that tone, "it's not that the dog doesn't love you," she continued delicately, and I knew a shoe was about to drop. "He just sees you as his equal."

Equal? Equal! How dare she! Did she know who I was? Obviously not!

I set the timer on the tanning room and sent her on her way. Equal. Ha!

Could such a thing be possible? I ran through the events of the last few weeks, honestly assessing my relationship with my dog. He came when I called him. He sat when I asked him some of the time. He stayed on the leash when we walked, and even though he pulled incessantly, every now and then he would look over his shoulder to see if I was following. He preferred my company over Cheryl's—she of the "insisting he sit and stay and not jump" school of thought.

Hmmm.

"So, how do I get Mr. Wilson to treat me like the boss?" I asked Christine when she was done tanning.

"You have to act like the boss."

"Like my wife?"

"Exactly."

I wasn't quite sure I liked this whole "acting like my wife, the boss" thing. Just who was the boss in my house? I am, that's who, and it was about time I started acting like it! The blow to my ego softened as each minute passed, and I let the idea into my head that perhaps I didn't have to be the alpha after all, but could still get the results I needed from Mr. Wilson. I needed for him to heel, not pull on the leash, sit, stay, and come. That was it. I was never a fan of doggie tricks without purpose, so if I could do what Cheryl had done, the experience would be better for everybody.

The Supreme Being had spoken, and he made sense. Sometimes talking to myself isn't such a bad idea after all.

Chapter 50

IT'S HIM!

Armed with my new resolve and a plan, I returned home. Mr. Wilson charged me, his entire countenance screaming, "IT'S HIM!" as soon as I walked through the door. As he began his charge, I turned my back. It killed me to do so, but progress needed to be made if we were to participate in the Providence Animal Rescue League's Pet Walk in just two weeks.

He flew into the back of my legs and tried to claw his way up my body.

"Any suggestions?" I asked Cheryl, who was nearby and exasperated.

"Yeah. Learn how to train him. He's fine; it's you who has the problem."

"I know."

She wasn't expecting that. We talked about training, alphas, betas, and whatevers, and watched some more YouTube videos from Zak George and a few others. I brushed up on what I thought I had learned from the book, *The Dog Whisperer* by Paul Owens. It's funny how much can be learned once you allow yourself to believe that you don't actually already know everything.

"I don't have to be mean," I said, as we watched Zak playing Frisbee with one of his dogs. "I can act like Mr. Wilson is my child, and I'm his dad."

"I think you're getting it," said Cheryl, and we watched some more lessons together.

I liked the "dad" thing much more than the "alpha." I was never comfortable with the whole alpha thing. I was just acting like the Supreme Being and everybody knew it. I didn't have to act to be a dad, though; I had learned how to do that already.

Danielle stopped by and brought her American Eskimo, Kaya, with her. We dog-sit for Kaya now and then and she's rather comfortable at our house. Mr. Wilson had grown rather comfortable with Kaya and proceeded to torture her. We let them out into the yard to play, which was more accurately Kaya begging to be let in and Mr. Wilson insisting Kaya stay out and play. Danielle and Kaya are inseparable, but their relationship wasn't accomplished without a lot of work. At one point, Danielle had to take Kaya to a doggie boot camp where, during a two-week period, she learned the rules of being a dog. The transformation truly was remarkable, and Kaya is now a welcome part of the family.

I missed having the kids living with us and wished we still lived in the house they spent most of their growing-up years in. It's different now when they stop by; it's like they are visiting us in our house rather than stopping at home to say hello. Their rooms are gone, their memories gone, their things packed into little plastic bins and stored in the basement.

But with loss there is always something to be learned, and while the places we spend our time may change, the people stay the same. Our pets may change, but knowing how delicate the things are that we hold dear, the time we get to spend with them has taken on greater importance.

Chapter 51

ZAK AND PAUL

The walk was coming quickly and we had lots of work to do. We had to learn how to behave in public, we had to raise money, and we had to find somebody to work at the tanning salon while we traipsed through Roger Williams Park. I was looking forward to the day, and the park is truly a beautiful place. My parents had their wedding pictures taken there, back in 1958, and it amazes me to this day just how beautiful my mother was. The pictures were taken at a place called the Temple to Music. For them, a marriage that lasted for nearly forty years got off to a glorious beginning. I liked looking at the pictures and thinking of what it was like for them—she only nineteen with four kids in her future that she had no idea were coming. With that kind of history on the sacred ground where we would present Mr. Wilson to the masses, we had better do it right!

Zak George's YouTube videos were instrumental in getting Mr. Wilson to walk without pulling. I used the videos to give me inspiration prior to beginning our training walks. Armed with knowledge passed from Zak to me through the miracle of the Internet, and some other inspiration in a more traditional form—namely *The Dog Whisperer* by Paul Owens and Norma Eckroate—we began what I believe will be a lifetime of understanding, training, and fun.

I never wanted to control my dogs, any of them, and Mr. Wilson even less so. I like to let living things live their way, at least when it doesn't interfere too much with my way, and the philosophy of positive training appealed to me. It can be confusing, the thought that an animal can be trained to do what he needs to do to have a better life by taking things away—but in a positive way—nearly drove me nuts until I was able to comprehend it.

If a dog—say an incredibly cute schnoodle named Mr. Wilson, for instance—wants to walk around the neighborhood and sniff and pee and say hello to the other dogs doing much the same, he needs to do so in a way that does not impinge on the rights of all the other dogs and dog walkers. By letting him live life his way—running around like a wild animal, jumping on people, scaring little dogs and even some big ones—the ultimate goal of true happiness is elusive. By learning and following some simple rules, all our lives are much more serene and satisfying.

Before we walk, I put his leash on him, but only after he sits and stays. When I take away the leash, he knows he will not be moving out the door and by not sitting, the leash will stay on its hook. If he doesn't stay, well then, the leash will just never be clasped onto his collar. When I take away something that he wants, he learns to do things that will result in a positive experience. Once the initial lessons are done—and he gets it 80 percent of the time—we can move out the door. At first, he did just that . . . and then I let my superior reasoning ability do its thing and reminded him that it was I who was taking him for a walk, therefore I needed to be the first out the door. It took a few tries, but within ten minutes he got it and sat until I said, "come."

Establishing the connection between us was one of the most wonderful experiences I have ever had in terms of relating with an animal. I loved every dog, cat, fish, hamster, and bug I have ever called my pet. But I never connected with them the way Mr. Wilson and I have connected. It was as though we learned to speak the same language, understood each other, and tried to do what it took to make our time together the best it could be. Had I not opened my mind to the possibility of such a thing, first through Cheryl's common sense, then Zak George's YouTube videos, and also with Paul Owens' book, the sense of satisfaction I now feel whenever I spend time with my dog would simply not exist. Zak's inherent goodness exudes from his videos, Paul's Eastern philosophy and good karma make sense to me, and Cheryl just kind of pulls it all together.

I wonder if the good feelings that come from the connection are somehow transmitted through the air and, on a molecular level, if such positive energy helps maintain the flow of goodness that I am certain keeps this world and universe moving toward the ultimate good, which has been described in a few different ways—Nirvana, Heaven, Valhalla, and more that I have no idea of. Sometimes everything comes together, and man and dog are one, and we walk without pulling. When cars come close, or a dog passes that wants nothing to do with us, what we have learned comes shining through.

I love walking a dog that listens. It gives me time to think. Perhaps what makes dogs such wonderful companions is their ability to listen without offering opinions of their own. They are silent sentinels; their emotional reactions to the world we share needs to be interpreted by us, and thus makes us more in tune to our surroundings, the people close to us, and the animals at the end of our leashes. Talk is cheap, and nobody knows that better than a dog. They don't have time to waste on idle chatter; their time on Earth is relatively short, so they fill their moments with quiet reflection and manage to comfort those around them when needed.

They can drive us nuts, too, but heck, they're dogs.

Chapter 52

THE KING, THE MOUSE, AND THE CHEESE

We brought Mr. Wilson to work with us and put up a sign offering a chance to win a free month's tanning to anybody who donated five dollars to the Providence Animal Rescue League. Mr. Wilson is always a hit at work; we keep him behind the desk, but with enough wiggle room to greet customers who wish to be greeted and a short enough leash to stop him just short of those who don't. Yes, there are those who don't. It's okay with Mr. Wilson, though. He gets the message rather quickly—once his friendship is offered and rebuffed, he circles back to his place behind the counter and lies down. If the person who chose to not greet him comes back, they are completely ignored by the four-legged clerk behind the desk. I wish Cheryl and I could get away with that; some people just don't give us the time of day. But they do spend their money at our place and deserve a hearty hello for that.

"Auntie" Elaine, Mr. Wilson's biggest fan, sometimes hides behind the counter when she sees us coming at shift change and surprises him, lavishing him with more cookies than he would normally see in a week. He's a smart cookie and knows that there might be something good behind the counter when we come to work, so he zeros in on the area as soon as we walk in the door. When Elaine is working, a love fest ensues and cookies are had, and I am forgotten completely. Eventually she has to go and take care of her cats, most of whom she has rescued, taken care of, spayed or neutered, and fed for years. She loves her animals and is one of the people whose efforts save so many from a miserable existence. If only there were more like her, there would be less suffering. I'm hoping that karma finds her, repays her kindness, and helps her through the battle she faces. The next few years are going to be difficult; she was diagnosed with stage four lymphoma and undergoes chemotherapy treatments on Mondays and Tuesdays, but always finds room in her heart for Mr. Wilson and her cats.

Elaine would rather raise money for homeless pets than she would for herself. She is no martyr; she has simply learned to live simple.

Within a few days, we had raised a respectable amount of money and the names of people who donated were put into a box until the day after the walk when we would draw the winner. As the days passed and the money and names grew, our training continued in earnest. I wanted Mr. Wilson shipshape for the Pet Walk, and we worked hard to make him presentable. We had never participated in such a thing, and I envisioned a million dogs all lined up, walking through the park like elephants with their tails in each other's mouths, nice and orderly and serene. Then a little cotton ball would show up like the mouse who ate the cheese and ruin the whole procession.

"You don't want to be a mouse, do you?" I asked him during one of our training walks. He looked over his shoulder from the "sit" position he assumed every time he pulled on the leash, and I stopped our forward motion and he shrugged his shoulders. I swear he understands me.

"Okay," I said happily, letting him know that as soon as tension was off the leash, we could move forward. The slack lasted for a few feet before tightening up, and again we stopped, and again he sat, and again I asked if he wanted to be a mouse.

And that was the way we learned to walk without pulling. First one foot, then two, then five, and before we knew it, a block. The whole process took only four or five days, and every day we need a little refresher, but that can be the best part of the walk. Just before embarking on our adventures, I crouch down to his eye level, point my index and middle fingers toward my eyes, then point at him, and the understanding that we are connected sinks in, and off we go.

"Heel" was next, and that took a little more effort, but eventually he figured it out. The pressure on the leash is the key; he knows that when there is no pressure, we go forward, and when he feels tightness around his neck, we stop. The concept is simple; carrying it out with consistency is the secret. A dog needs structure, just like a man, and the two of us benefited greatly from our routine. I feel better with a plan, even if the plan is a simple thing barely formulated in the back of my head, swimming around with all of the other half-baked plans. But this time, things were different. We had a goal, and the goal of walking with hundreds of other dogs without creating a scene was obtainable, I just knew it. So we walked, we trained, we planned, and we were ready.

Chapter 53

THE WALK

Our fundraising efforts had raised a little over five hundred dollars. Not bad for a rescue dog, Elaine, and a couple of wounded old people who still thought they were young. The Pet Walk began at10:00 a.m., but I had no intention of being on time and hanging around waiting for the fun to start. The real fun was planned for noon, when the parade around the park began; the rest was simply registration and socializing. I had done the registration the night before and was still a little worried about socializing, so we held off until the last minute.

Cheryl drove us to the park and, after a brief recon expedition, decided the best place to leave us was right in the middle of things. Mr. Wilson was completely over-stimulated. He jumped from his car seat and nearly hanged himself. Great start. I extricated him, he settled down a bit, and we watched a long procession of dogs and their owners stroll past us. Cheryl had to move the car out of the way, so we said our goodbyes, and she drove away to find a parking spot, hopefully somewhere where she could see all the dogs marching past her and find some happiness from watching them. Mr. Wilson and I were on our own.

"Okay, boy, here we go," I said to him, after crouching down and getting his attention. For his part, he was doing quite well, and I noticed that he was a little timid, the exact opposite of what I had expected. A few people dragged their dogs in the opposite direction, obviously ill-prepared for the event. They had to slink into the background while the well-trained pooches marched on. The majority of dogs and owners had begun the walk and we were behind the pack, but I knew the park like the back of my hand and knew a few shortcuts. We cut through a field in front of the Temple to Music and ended up smack dab in the middle of the fun.

"That wasn't cheating, Mr. Wilson. I cleared the shortcut with the walk administrator yesterday when I registered." He looked at me dubiously and kept on walking.

We found a peaceful break in the lineup and took our place, walking in rhythm with all the rest of the people and their pets. Wilson was wonderful—didn't pull on the leash, and heeled when I asked him to. A few people passed us, and a few butts were sniffed, but there was no insane greeting like there is on our neighborhood walks, where it's as if the dogs had never encountered another of their species and absolutely, positively have to make contact or the future of the world as they know it will be in jeopardy.

Perhaps there is a group consciousness between large groups of dogs, some unseen intelligence that allows them to behave while grouped together in great numbers. Maybe the power of those numbers calms them and puts them in the right frame of mind to be able to walk with their owners and enjoy the moment without going mad over every dog they see. Maybe they are simply overwhelmed.

Whatever the reason, I was awestruck with serenity, as hundreds of dogs walked together, and there was no fighting, no foolish behavior, and not a bark to be heard. That amazed me the most; put two dogs together on my street and the bark fest begins, then the circling, finally the sniffing and acceptance. Here, the acceptance came without all of the preliminaries, and it was a great bonding experience.

People with dogs, especially during something like a Pet Walk, are kinder than people without. A kinship exists between people walking their dogs. It's as if an agreement is made between beast and person, and if they are to be leashed together then they had better make the best of it. A few people walked the park by themselves, or with other people, but they were obviously missing what we were, and they looked longingly at the trail of happy pets and pet owners as we took over the park. Even less fortunate were the people stuck in their cars, looking longingly out their windows as we walked past, wishing they could be a part of the procession. I'm probably nuts, and the "other" people barely noticed us, but I like thinking we were the special people, at least for that moment. Something about walking a dog makes me think that everybody else wants to be doing exactly what I am.

It occurred to me that I actually was doing exactly what I wanted to be doing, and that doesn't happen nearly often enough. I had a moment of tranquility while in the midst of what I thought would be controlled chaos, and I walked off to the side of the road with Mr. Wilson to enjoy the moment. A huge statue of a man on a horse sat at the edge of a forest, surrounded by a wrought iron fence, sword raised, his face determined, horse rearing, his proud countenance indicative of a person in charge of his life and headed in the right direction. I saw up close what I had previously only observed from a moving vehicle as I sped past it. The man on the horse was General Casimir Pulaski, a Revolutionary War hero who was mortally wounded on October 9, 1779, during the Battle of Savannah and died at the age of thirty-two. The beauty of the art and the message of the artist opened up to me as I was drawn closer and I wondered why I had never bothered to see it before. I had passed the statue thousands of times while responding in Rescue 1 to emergencies in and around the park, but never allowed myself the luxury of appreciating my surroundings. Instead, I saw the road before me as a means to an end, never considering I might enjoy the ride. Life is a journey, and you can travel the super-highway and rush toward the end or take a side road and enjoy the view. I realized then how fortunate I was to have found Exit 89 in Connecticut and be given the chance to slow down and enjoy the ride. I took a moment, closed my eyes, and silently thanked General Pulaski. Mr. Wilson sat next to me and looked to the trees, hungry for birds.

We rejoined the walkers, feeling great, and happy to be part of something I would have never even considered had I not been given a scrappy little dog named Wilson. Cheryl knew exactly what we needed, and I saw her in the distance, sitting in our car, which she had parked at the finish line. She saw us, and a connection was made. The three of us finished the walk together.

Chapter 54

THE REUNION

"Two big weekends in a row. We're going to need a vacation!" I said as we drove toward Connecticut and Cheryl's annual family reunion. Mr. Wilson sat in the back seat, nestled in his car carrier, looking like a white Toto on his way to Oz.

"That's where we got Wilson," said Cheryl, as we drove past the Route 395 on-ramp.

"Seems like we've had him forever," I said, glancing behind me and seeing that he was okay.

"Things worked out better than I could have imagined," said Cheryl. "I was worried that he would be a jerk."

"So was I."

Mr. Wilson listened from his perch.

"I love having him around. It's amazing; I've never gotten mad at him."

"Even when he eats the cat food?"

"Nope."

"Kills the birds?"

"He hasn't gotten one in a while."

"Not from lack of trying. How about when he pees on the rug?"

"I never liked that rug, and he doesn't do it anymore."

"He's just a good dog."

"Yeah, he is."

That is what is so amazing. He is just a good dog. That's it. Forget about the labels, the pedigrees and lack thereof, the abused rescue dog story, the stigma of the designer dog and all of that. What mattered most—the only thing that mattered, really—was that he was simply a good dog. And we were simply good people who loved him.

We were among the last to arrive for the reunion, and the park was full of people picnicking, playing Frisbee, running around in the sun or sitting in the shade. A large group off to the side of the park gathered around cousins Lisa and Dennis's mobile home. Next to a quickly running stream full of frogs were the rest of Cheryl's cousins, aunts, uncles, and in-laws; the older ones sitting, the younger ones taking care of the older ones, and the very youngest ones running and playing without a care in the world. Mr. Wilson made himself at home and quickly ingratiated himself with a group of five- to ten-year-old girls who happily took the leash from me and led him to every corner of the ten-acre park. Every now and then, he and I would make eye contact, sometimes from ten feet away, other times well over a hundred. The connection between us never ebbed, and we stayed at the park for hours. The girls adopted him, and he was the center of attention and he loved every minute of it.

We ate, and ate, and ate some more, and talked and had some laughs and caught up on things, and before long it was time to go.

The girls reluctantly gave Mr. Wilson back, and we were happy to have him. He was through with his new friends, exhausted, and happy to be back with us. We said our goodbyes and made those plans that are always made at reunions to get together before next year, all the while knowing that most of us would not see each other until next year and the next reunion.

It was a great day, and I'm glad we went, because all too often we have let our difficulties get in the way of enjoying our lives and the people in it. Getting places while battling multiple sclerosis is difficult, but not impossible. Being part of a large gathering while not able to participate fully is frustrating and potentially heartbreaking, but better than not participating at all. And going to a park on a beautiful late summer's day beats working overtime every time.

"That was fun," Cheryl said, as we drove away toward home.

"Yeah it was," I answered.

Mr. Wilson slept, his body sinking low in his car seat, a gentle snoring coming over the sides the only evidence of his presence.

We drove in comfortable silence for a few miles, feeling the gentle peaks and valleys in the road as we sped over it, eventually driving past the on-ramp toward Route 395 where only a few months ago we met Wilson. We silently acknowledged the landmark with a simultaneous squeeze of our hands, which had somehow become entwined.

EPILOGUE

We have a good dog, and we are grateful. But a good dog does not a wonderful life make. Without love, compassion, and a lot of gratitude and understanding, the greatest dog in the world wouldn't make a bit of difference in our, or anybody's, life. Seeing, understanding, and appreciating the kindness embodied in Mr. Wilson is the most important aspect of fully enjoying life with him. Countless great dogs live out their lives in shelters or worse, their inherent goodness going unnoticed by the very people their species has become dependent on.

The quality of a dog's life is almost completely at the mercy of humanity. Without us, they would have no choice but to be wild animals and, through the process of evolution, have become poor ones. They have evolved from their ancestral roots as wolves, fully capable of living in the wild and thriving, into domestic partners that are attractive to humans. Their looks, their smell, the sounds they make, the love they emit, and the loyalty that resides within them make them welcome additions to our homes where we take care of all their needs in return for nothing more than their company. Even the most poorly trained dog brings with him a certain charm that captivates the most hard-hearted among us.

It is our responsibility to be capable providers. They are doing their job; we need to do a better job at ours.

Mr. Wilson is truly a gift. It is up to us to accept him as such, nurture his goodness, and let him become part of our lives without allowing him to overrun it. Many a good dog becomes little more than furniture after a few years, or a pest: cast off, chained in the yard and ignored, or treated as a chore rather than a partner. Training is the key, and it need not be a life's work.

Sit. Stay. Come. Down. Four simple words, with meaning anybody can teach and any dog can learn, have the ability to make our relationship with our dogs what they are meant to be: simple, fun, nurturing, and harmonious. It takes time, patience, and commitment, but the effort is small and the rewards are great.

Somewhere a dog every bit as good as Mr. Wilson sits alone, chained to a tree, stuck in a tiny cage delivering litter after litter of puppies, or waiting on death row for the end to come. He's waiting for the human contact he needs to thrive and survive to come along and allow him to be free, both physically and spiritually, and to join the human race as a partner, friend, pet, and companion.

But he can't wait forever.

And neither can we.

"That was a good day," said Cheryl, once we were home, unpacked, and settled in.

"Seems like there's been a lot of those lately," I said, and Cheryl smiled.

We looked at Mr. Wilson, who had retreated to his crate. With his head rested on his favorite toy, he looked first at me, then at Cheryl, fluttered his eyes, and drifted off to sleep.